Sarah, you channeled me in the first two paragraphs. Thank you for clarifying my thoughts! I am ready to get this little book and see how it will affect my future with Young Living.

Shannon Woods

Oh my gosh it's soooooo good!!! I can't stop thinking about the introduction where you said, "your plate is overflowing." I realized this business didn't add to my plate, it's a whole new plate to balance everything in my life!!! Thank you for sharing Gary's love for us!!! And the scripts... so easy to use and to read!!! I LOVE the book!!! #amazonbestseller

Julie M. Finnemore

I read this in 42 minutes top to bottom. I now have a new way to train all my Distributors, Stars, and frozen upper leadership! It's hard to believe—but the master of Young Living business writing—Sarah Harnisch- has done it again. Everyone needs this book in their arsenal of training material. In her usual news anchor style, Sarah trains skillfully, but in as few words as possible; simplifying a Young Living business for those that need it fast. I CAN launch a leader in two hours. The power of Gameplan ~~~~ the ~~~~ ~~ ~~~ ~~~'s is what we have been w

Sheridan

A shout out to the Diamonds willing to preview this book:

Stacie Malkus	Jeanna Lichtenberger
Carol Yeh-Garner	Faith Teo
Teri Secrest	Oli and Ellen Wenker
Jessica Petty	Cathy Alegre
Marcella Vonn Harting	Sandi Weldon Boudreau
Chelsa Bruno	Ryan and Jenny McManus
Penny Enriques Miranda	Shannon Hudson
Mary Shea Buck	Laura Kellogg Peiffer
Lisa Blackstock	James McDonald
Amanda Friedl	Tina Dailey Ceisla
Carla Green	Darlene Weir
Sophia Sharpe	Diane Mora

And to the powerful editing team, for months of work:

Debbie Wheeler, Katie Burl, Jennifer Wise, Penny Sorokes, Mercedes Thurston, Judy Bofah

Layout and cover design by: Cory Rucker

THE ESSENTIAL
GAMEPLAN

Your *Ignite* Business
In 2 Hours

Sarah Harnisch
Young Living Diamond

Oil Ability
TEAM.COM

DEDICATION

For Domenica, the dairy farmer that I met just once, with love.

May you never work another 80-hour week again. I wrote this whole book with you in my head, hearing your voice and all your valid concerns in my mind as I typed. You CAN do this despite the very hard burden you carry. Your farm and your passions will not be lost if you love Young Living too. The small moments in your day are enough to go all the way to the top if you are consistent. May the simplicity of these words guide you as you build to Royal, worthy friend.

You are worth fighting for.

For Royal Crown Diamond Darlene Weir.

Who showed up at my door and said "Gameplan is EXACTLY what I need for my team. But can you make it smaller?" You have always challenged me to hear needs that I have missed. You see people in a way that is so unique. I am stronger because I know you. Your joy and your fight forever inspire me! You are a gift to all of Young Living, and you are a gift to me.

To D. Gary Young –

Oh Gary! I can never repay you for what you've given my family! May this modest book be used to get oils into every home in the world as we duplicate leaders by the tens of thousands across the earth. Your mission has not been forgotten. If I had just a few drops of your gift of loving people, it would be so easy to train others to share. There was never any fear in you. You always saw the good and never the bad. My voice has more grace and more mercy because of your kindness and love of all people.

Ignite Table of Contents

Introduction

You are not completely sure what a Young Living business is; and you absolutely don't want to sell to your friends. You know what that feels like. Yet you feel a tug toward oils because you believe in kicking poison out of your home and replacing it with natural products. You have seen what oils have done to your friends' homes; and you believe in them, but you can't afford them.

Maybe you're starting simply from a place where this little book is your first introduction to Young Living. You're unfamiliar with oils, but you need some extra income in your home. If it grew into something crazy like a Diamond income, that opportunity would change everything for your family—but you'd be happy with even a little. Things are tight. Stress is high. You need relief. The pressure valve must be released because you feel you are drowning. You have been subsistence living for far too long. Each paycheck is gone before it makes it to your savings account.

You have an interest in this, but you truly don't have time. Your plate is overflowing. If you're going to learn how to do this, you need to learn it fast. You can't watch 50 videos and do hundreds of hours of training. You don't have money to invest. You have babies at home, work that's time consuming, limited income, and nothing else will fit in that small space. You feel that you have little to give and need a high yield for your time.

You may not be in any of those categories. You may be the weary builder that knows you WANT this. You're the one who has tried over and over and is overwhelmed. You have been sitting at the same rank for a very long time. You need something SIMPLE to understand how to do this, without all the bells and whistles. You need a system. And you need to get leaders off the ground, ready to launch in a single afternoon. You need them to catch the passion, take action, and run! You need self-starters.

You are holding the answer to all those questions in your hand right now!!

You have been heard!

My name is Sarah. I live in a little town in the mountains in up-state New York. I'm a mom of five; and I started in the same place where you are right now, just a short time ago. I juggled a full-time job anchoring news at 4am - atop a seven-hour homeschool day when I began this business. After living in the government projects for 12 years, I had little to offer anyone when I launched this thing. I'm here to tell you, standing before you as a Young Living Diamond (just two years after my starter kit showed up on my door), that this *can* be done! It can be done with no background in sales, marketing, network marketing or business. It can be done if you're juggling one, two, or more jobs. It can be done if you work an overnight shift. It can be done if you're caring for aging parents or children with special needs. It can be done if your body is adrenally shot. It can be done if you have little ones and work as a stay at home mom. It can be done if you moved across the country and don't know a single person in the town where you live. It can be done if you've blasted through the people you know and no one is listening. It can be done without making cold calls and feeling "salesy". It can be done if you've tried network marketing before and failed. It can be done with only minutes each day. It can be done if your bank account is overdrawn. It can be done when nothing else fits on your plate. It can be done if your self-image is crushed and you think you have nothing to offer anyone. It can be done if you've been abused, hurt, and left behind. It can be done if you are broken.

You see... I was all those things. I started in every one of those places. I felt I had nothing to pour out. That's ok! That is the perfect place to start, because the only place to go from here is up.

Let me pour some hope into you in that dark place, because there IS a way out! You don't have to stay there anymore. You don't need to be tired. When you are tired, you can't do what the Lord has called and created you to do. You have nothing to give. The thing is... that's a lie! You DO have something to give. You must crawl from the place where you are and not believe the things in your head. Even if you've been there for decades, it's not too late to move. You ARE enough. God made no mistakes when He put you together.

In this itty-bitty book, I'm going to walk you through how I did it and how the Diamonds before me pulled it off. It comes down to **loving people and not giving up**. If I can train you in that small space, we will grow together; and you can build something that will bless your family for generations. You can build a willable income that can be left to them, so they will not have to walk the road of exhaustion you have walked.

I'm not going to hand you fish; I'm going to teach you how to fish. It will happen quickly! You will be fully trained on the basics by tonight. If you're using this to train a leader, you can get them off the ground and ready to launch their business in one afternoon. This book is a powerhouse. It's all the critical pieces of the *Gameplan* book in a miniature form.

Best of all... you're not going to sell to *anyone*. You're going to teach them how to care for their families. You're an educator. Every family you touch will have their lives forever changed for the better.

Start by peeking at the image below. The Income Disclosure Statement tells you where this goes. This "Ignite" book is hard core Young Living Business training, "nuts-and-bolts" style, that will get you on that chart. If you rinse and repeat the steps in this book consistently without distraction or excuses, you have all you need to get through the first four ranks and beyond in Young Living. Are you ready? Here we go!

YOUNG LIVING 2017 WORLDWIDE

WORLDWIDE INCOME STATISTICS FOR
JANUARY - DECEMBER 2017

WHAT ARE MY EARNING OPPORTUNITIES?
This document provides statistical, fiscal data about the average member income and information about achieving various ranks.

DISTRIBUTOR

PERCENTAGE OF ALL BUSINESS BUILDERS	MONTHLY INCOME				ANNUALIZED AVERAGE INCOME	AVERAGE MONTHS TO ACHIEVE RANK		
	Lowest	Highest	Median	Average		Low	Average	High
33.3%	$0	$725	$15	$26	$312	N/A	N/A	N/A

STAR

PERCENTAGE OF ALL BUSINESS BUILDERS	MONTHLY INCOME				ANNUALIZED AVERAGE INCOME	AVERAGE MONTHS TO ACHIEVE RANK		
	Lowest	Highest	Median	Average		Low	Average	High
41.02%	$0	$932	$58	$75	$906	1	12	267

SENIOR STAR

PERCENTAGE OF ALL BUSINESS BUILDERS	MONTHLY INCOME				ANNUALIZED AVERAGE INCOME	AVERAGE MONTHS TO ACHIEVE RANK		
	Lowest	Highest	Median	Average		Low	Average	High
15.46%	$2	$5,531	$195	$235	$2,819	1	19	255

EXECUTIVE

PERCENTAGE OF ALL BUSINESS BUILDERS	MONTHLY INCOME				ANNUALIZED AVERAGE INCOME	AVERAGE MONTHS TO ACHIEVE RANK		
	Lowest	Highest	Median	Average		Low	Average	High
6.62%	$34	$13,210	$425	$502	$6,028	1	25	254

SILVER

PERCENTAGE OF ALL BUSINESS BUILDERS	MONTHLY INCOME				ANNUALIZED AVERAGE INCOME	AVERAGE MONTHS TO ACHIEVE RANK		
	Lowest	Highest	Median	Average		Low	Average	High
2.55%	$229	$29,248	$1,698	$2,088	$25,059	1	32	252

GOLD

PERCENTAGE OF ALL BUSINESS BUILDERS	MONTHLY INCOME				ANNUALIZED AVERAGE INCOME	AVERAGE MONTHS TO ACHIEVE RANK		
	Lowest	Highest	Median	Average		Low	Average	High
0.57%	$1,506	$48,630	$4,541	$5,666	$67,995	2	49	263

PLATINUM

PERCENTAGE OF ALL BUSINESS BUILDERS	MONTHLY INCOME				ANNUALIZED AVERAGE INCOME	AVERAGE MONTHS TO ACHIEVE RANK		
	Lowest	Highest	Median	Average		Low	Average	High
0.18%	$4,375	$90,275	$11,057	$13,872	$166,468	5	58	243

DIAMOND

PERCENTAGE OF ALL BUSINESS BUILDERS	MONTHLY INCOME				ANNUALIZED AVERAGE INCOME	AVERAGE MONTHS TO ACHIEVE RANK		
	Lowest	Highest	Median	Average		Low	Average	High
0.07%	$6,256	$163,387	$27,972	$35,348	$424,178	7	70	251

CROWN DIAMOND

PERCENTAGE OF ALL BUSINESS BUILDERS	MONTHLY INCOME				ANNUALIZED AVERAGE INCOME	AVERAGE MONTHS TO ACHIEVE RANK		
	Lowest	Highest	Median	Average		Low	Average	High
0.01%	$28,492	$231,397	$53,539	$64,477	$773,724	16	85	256

ROYAL CROWN DIAMOND

PERCENTAGE OF ALL BUSINESS BUILDERS	MONTHLY INCOME				ANNUALIZED AVERAGE INCOME	AVERAGE MONTHS TO ACHIEVE RANK		
	Lowest	Highest	Median	Average		Low	Average	High
0.02%	$50,770	$326,334	$132,828	$144,351	$1,734,608	17	97	230

Fighting When You Have No Fight

A Note from Sarah
Before You Start "Ignite"

Your story may be so much worse than mine. Your feet may have scaled mountains and your hands worked so hard that I can't imagine the places you have been. My journey is so small compared to most. My desire and my strategy for sharing my journey is to shine some hope on you. Because without hope, there's no movement. There's no dreaming and there's no way out.

I'm not going to promise you that any network marketing company is going to make you rich. I'm not going to promise you early retirement and cars and vacations. I am going to tell you that with the right type of hard work, (concentrated, strategic relationship building,) this can turn you the other direction. At the very least, you will have a head and a heart full of ideas, a lot of momentum, and an idea of the way out. At most, it can go as far as you want it to go—even all the way to Royal Crown Diamond. I can count on one hand the number of things that have truly changed the course of my life: my Lord and Savior, my precious husband, my kids, my friends and mentors and family, and Young Living.

You see, I lived in poverty for 12 years in Illinois. Half of those years were in the projects. The photos above are from my time there with four of my five kids. There were cockroaches on the floor as we slept. We had cinderblock walls. At my first radio job, I made $21 dollars a month in take-home pay and worked at a deli when I wasn't at the station for minimum wage. There were many nights that we went to bed with our jackets on as our power was shut off, and I saw my breath as I slept. There were days that the food pantry was out of food, and we lived on chocolate pudding. This was my life, day in and day out, with no way out. I looked at my kids and wanted better for them but had no idea how to get there. I lived check to check from the time I got married at 19 until I was 39 years old, scrambling, stumbling, and surviving.

What if I were to tell you that you don't need to stay there? What if I were to tell you that if you could learn the art of telling your story with passion, meeting people's needs, and loving on them where they are—that the simple act of getting over fear and loving people can build something amazing?

Young Living was a lot of work! It took me 288 classes to get to Diamond. I had no network to pull from. I didn't know a lot of people because I'd moved 750 miles from my hometown. But I believed in oils. I saw them work. I know that people want a way of taking care of their families that doesn't include a list of poisonous ingredients. And I knew if I met people in that place, that this may go somewhere. Maybe I'd get some oils for free. Maybe I'd get to freedom.

Both have happened for me—and I'm never looking back. The part of my life in the projects is over forever. I share my past with you because I truly believe we forget to dream. We give up. We get overwhelmed and exhausted. And we watch life instead of living it. At worst, you'll read this book and draw a goal in the sand. At best, it will be a life-changing course correction. When you get to a place where you are so broken and lost, it's sometimes hard to see the way out. I remember that space like it was yesterday. And I want so much more for you!

You are at a fork in the road. Someone has placed Ignite in your hands because they deeply believe in you. They want to invest in you. They have seen where this can go if you roll up your sleeves. And they want better for you. Nothing happens until you dream and see it first.

Let's start in that place together. No expectations, but big dreams. It's always safe to dream! When you forget to dream, and you forget to plan, your feet will stay stuck in the miry mud. The only way out is to move. This book will train you on exactly what I did to break free.

Will our paths look the same? Perhaps not. But perhaps... so. I can promise you one thing: if you stay where you are, you'll have the same list of frustrations ten years from now. And everything will remain unchanged. Here's the thing: I believe that this is not a year of the same old stuff for you. This is the year of hope.

Do not forget that you are worthy of the crown.

So take my hand, and let's do this together. It's worth the work!

With great love,

Sarah

CHAPTER 1

SCRIPT. KIT. HUMAN.

Young Living is a lifestyle. It's so much more than selling a starter kit. When you catch the vision of where this goes, it will change everything about how you care for your family. I promise you with everything in me, you will never look back. You don't use Thieves Cleaner and then return to your other cleaning products. Your original cleaning supplies, air fresheners, plug ins, and candles will start giving you headaches as your body realizes they were never meant to be in your home in the first place.

You cannot use oils to Band-Aid a lifestyle decision. You CAN, however, take small steps to start rethinking the products in your home, such as: cleaning supplies (such as: Thieves cleaner, laundry soap, and hand soap); personal care kits (with items such as: Cool Azul Pain cream and Thieves Cough Drops and Young Living Acne Treatment and Mineral Sunscreen lotion); bathroom products (such as: ART Gentle Cleanser face wash and Thieves toothpaste); food (such as: Einkorn Flakes cereal and granola,

NingXia Wolfberry juice and Vitality internal oils); and supplements (such as: Super C, Multi Greens, Detoxzyme, and Nitro).

This might all seem overwhelming, but it's a process. It took 12 years for me to kick everything out of my cabinets. It started with 24 years of migraines and brain bleeds until I changed my diet. I cut all sugar, gluten, and dairy products. That led me to evaluate the bright blue dish soap on my counter... and question if there was any connection to that and the way my kids behaved after washing all their dishes in dye. One small step at a time, over a period of years, I kicked toxic chemicals to the curb in my home. It's not instant. You may have many things in your cabinets right now that you're emotionally tied to, are a part of your daily habit, or just don't have the income to swap out. That's ok! I have not met a Diamond yet that had pure cabinets the minute they started this business. You start from the place that most convicts you. Perhaps it's your laundry soap, counter cleaner, or shampoo. Always teach from that humble, real, honest place. People will connect to you because of your journey, not because of your perfection. The starting place with Young Living is to train the lifestyle.

Your task is to train people how to start the simple swap and how to start removing things that are toxic from their cabinets, replacing them with Young Living products, one at a time. The way to do it is overly simple. You might question my system, but I swear to you, it works. For every three 101 classes I taught, I allowed myself to teach a "specialty" class to pre-existing members. I taught an Oola class, an Oils of the Bible class, a Feelings Kit class, in order to train on Essential Rewards. I always kept my ratios three to one. Seventy-five percent of your time must be spent prospecting, and not teaching to your pre-existing team if you want to stay in a pattern of growth. Don't get distracted with teaching classes that don't lead to one of the four starter kits. That's where the longevity is on your team. Give your 101 classes any pretty title you want and teach them in a way that resonates with you. There are so many good ways of sharing the 101 script. Whichever method you use, skip the bells and whistles, and keep it simple so you don't overwhelm upcoming leaders. I stuck with that method for two years, collected 800 leaders, and grew my team to over 4,000 in the month we made Diamond. This is the pattern: script, kit, people, repeat.

I provided you with the script at the end of this book. You will need a Young Living Premium Starter kit for demonstrating the oils in your classes. I recommend the Premium Starter Kit with 12 oils and a Desert Mist diffuser. You'll be trained on how to find the people in the next chapter, as well as how to communicate the need for getting toxins out of their homes in a way that isn't "salesy." I just wanted you to see the purpose and the method first.

If you can do that one weekly act of connecting with people, you will have everything you need to blow this up. It's not about thousands of dollars in training or hundreds of hours of your time. It doesn't take 40 hours a week to do this. It takes a script, a kit, and people. I taught the script at the end of this book 288 times. On my 289th class, we hit Diamond. Will it look that way for you? It depends how consistent you are. It depends on your ability to connect and train from a place of humility, love, and compassion. It depends if you can emotionally detach yourself from the sale of the kit, and not wear every response as a banner of how success-ful you are. In this business, the more no's you get, the harder you are working. A rank up happens brick by brick. The more often you get the script in front of faces, the faster you will rank. And it will change your life forever. A year or two of consistent hustle could mean a completely different future... if you take this seriously.

"Is it really as simple as reading a script to people, showing them the kit, and signing them up under me???" Yes! That one action, rinsed and repeated, over and over again without distractions, is what got me to Diamond. How you share is not as important as *that* you share. Many have been successful reading the script online, using textable classes, training on Instagram, doing vendor

events, or carrying purple bags. There are many ways of sharing. It all comes down to the basic, simple, system of connecting with people. That's what I'm going to train you on inside and out, and upside down in this tiny book. Then you can go out and practice it immediately and get results; because this works.

Young Living may feel like a large commitment from an outside perspective. How do you dig out, and build a business, *and* juggle all the plates you have to carry? Let me speak to that. <u>You don't need to start this thing with a goal of going to the top</u>. Your goals right now, whatever size, are *absolutely perfect*. They will change like the sand in the waves on the beach as you rank. Don't look at the ocean. Focus on the very next step that you want to be. You don't get to Royal Crown Diamond by staring at a sea of endless to-do lists. You get there with small consistent goals. Block the size of the journey from your mind and focus on why you want this. That reason will give you the drive to do the next thing.

Do you want your oils for free? That's a big enough goal in itself right now. Do you want your closest friends and family on Thieves instead of toxic cleaning products? That goal is enough in this moment. Do you want to be able to give generously, anonymously, and not always be on the edge financially? What about leaving financial peace for your kids? All of those goals are possible with Young Living. You cannot out dream your business. For now, start with the next thing and the next thing only. The next thing is reading this book to the very last page.

Step one is to practice one of the two scripts in the back of this book. Now go read it five times in the mirror. Check the boxes off below as you read it each time. You don't need to do it in one sitting.

101 Script Practice ☐ ☐ ☐ ☐ ☐

102 Script Practice ☐ ☐ ☐ ☐ ☐

Next, jot down your personal story below by answering the following questions:

- Who invited me to my first oils class?

- What was my journey? Did I get the kit right away? Did I believe in oils?

- What was my "wow" moment? What story got me with oils? (It can be in your family, or something that you witnessed.)

- Are there any oils in the Premium Starter Kit that got my attention, and why?

- Why do I believe wholeheartedly in Young Living?

_____

_____

_____

_____

_____

_____

_____

Chapter 2

What My First Class Looked Like

One of the best decisions I made before my business truly took off was to encourage my friends and family first. Sign your circle. You may not know a lot of people, but you likely know someone who knows a lot of people. Show them what oils can do. I'll be the first to tell you that preaching to Nazareth is the hardest place. Some of your family members may be the last to sign. My dad and sister are not involved in Young Living. My mom, however, has Platinum volume and my other sister has acheived Gold. My sister-in-law is Gold; and my brother is Executive. The heads of several of my legs (a leg is a person and a team) are Silvers, Golds, and Platinums; and they are my best friends. You want to carry your family with you as move forward with your goal. If they're willing to listen in the very beginning, I love to place them at the top of my organization whether they will build or not, soley just to bless them. Their one requirement? They need to spend 100PV to get their paycheck every month. That is all. Sign friends and family and take them with you.

Try to keep your story around three to five minutes. Once you get good at telling it in person, you'll be able to shave it to one or two minutes to share quickly when meeting with people in a random hallway or in passing conversation. That's your intro to get them to come to a class. That's your power story. That's your why. If you don't have a "why" yet, it's ok! Start with toxic-free living. That's a place where you can connect with people with like-minded views. You'll build your story as you use more and more Young Living products and have "wow" moments with them. You can't learn if you aren't playing with the products.

How do I actually find people?? The first person I want you to focus on is your best friend or your mom. Pick the people closest to you. If you had a store in your hometown, who would be the first people to show up? Start in that place. Do you know someone that would be incredibly blessed by the business or that has an amazing work ethic? Do you know someone you'd LOVE doing the business alongside? Start with them. The nice thing about this is that you get to choose your team for your business.

When I say, "start with them", what does that look like? Share your oils story that we practiced on the opposite page. Share why chemical-free living matters so much. If you're not sure why it matters so much, review the 102 script at the end of this book: Toxin Free Life. I've included both the 101 and 102 scripts at the end of this book simply because some people aren't ready to start with oils. It's too foreign to them. Begin with Thieves. That's a comfortable starting place, because most people will agree that their chemical cleaners are toxic. Pull a couple of stats from the 102 class, and use those as your talking points. For example, "one in three men will develop cancer in the United States after the age of 60. One in five women will develop cancer after age 60 as well. The American Cancer Society says only 5-10 percent of all cancer cases are caused by our genes. What does that mean? It's environmental. It's what we're allowing into our homes. We MUST take this seriously. Only you are the gatekeeper of your home. Come to my home Friday night and I'll train you how to protect your home."

Once you've shared why this lifestyle matters, invite them to your home. It may be just you and your bestie. That's ok. For the first class, if it's a single person in the room and you're using them to warm up to the idea of teaching, there's nothing wrong with that. When you first begin, every person you sign, sign them under you.

"Huh"? How do you do that?

When you got your starter kit, you were assigned a member number. That is the number you use, like a referral number, for people to get a kit and become one of your team members. As your team grows, I'll train you on a simple strategy where to sign them so you can rank up more swiftly. For now, at the very beginning, every person is signed under you. To obtain your member number, go to youngliving.com and click on "sign in". You created a login name and password when you purchased your kit. Enter it online and it will take you to your "back office". It's called the Virtual Office. The first page you see is your dashboard.

It looks something like this, and has all your stats at a glance:

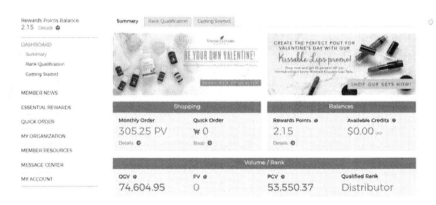

We'll go over what all that means in a later chapter. For now, to get your member number, click on "My Organization". You will see your name and "member ID." That's the number you use as a sponsor and enroller at the very beginning of your business. As you start to strategize your team, you'll use a different number for being a sponsor, and will place people under others to create legs. For this first class, and until you have at least 10 people signed under you, use your own member ID number for both sponsor and enroller every single time someone gets a kit.

You can also use your member ID number and password, if you forget your login name. If you are not able to remember either and are unable to log into the Virtual Office, call Member Services at this number: (1-800-371-3515); and they will get your member ID number for you.

You now have your number. You know how to log into the Virtual Office. Ok... we're ready to go!

Grab the script. Grab a human. Share the story I had you write out. End with the Bold Close script at the end of this book. Make sure you have a laptop or computer ready. Open to the "youngliving. com" website so they can order a kit. End your class with the story of your journey. "I started my journey with a Young Living starter kit. This is where I recommend that you start too. The Young Living Premium Starter Kit is the only thing on the website that is half off. I am a frugal momma. I like stuff half off! This kit is loaded with tools for respiratory support, digestive support, immune support, and everything else you need in a one-stop-shop to learn oiling. Let's learn this together."

The next step: they sit down, order the kit; and you put the book "Fearless" in their hands. In a little over a week, you have a new oiler with a fully stocked kit on your team.

Start sharing with one person, then two or three more. If you're bold and have a lot of Valor oil (for courage!), host twelve for your first class. The most important thing is that you are consistently sharing. At first, it may be your friends and family because they are most apt to listen right out of the gate. Also, because you want Young Living in their homes more than anyone else you know. As you gain confidence with the script, you'll branch out to friends of friends, coworkers, people at your place of worship, places where you volunteer, parents on the soccer field, customers at Walmart, patrons at the post office, and anyone else that will listen.

Still not confident? Accept the coffee house challenge. Sit in a Starbucks or Panera until you have struck up a conversation with three perfect strangers. Ask them their favorite menu item or where they are from. Do not talk oils. After, come home and read the script to a friend. That simple act of realizing you can connect with people (even those you do not know) is enough to build confidence.

That may sound scary right now. It's simply learning how to connect with people. When that skill is mastered, you have 100% market share. Anyone will listen, because you have what they need: toxic-free living. It's simpler to share the benefits of Young Living than it is to share pots, pans, and leggings (that you have to invest $5000 in product to stock in your garage), makeup, or supplements. Not everyone NEEDS those things, but everyone NEEDS oils. Your task is to show them that they need it because it will change everything for them. I have completely altered how I care for my kids, how I clean, and what we use in the rooms of our home because of two words spoken to me in 2014: Young Living.

Chapter 3

How Do I Find People?

Ok Sarah... I get it. You take the script. You take the kit. You read the script in front of humans and pass around the kit. You get oils in their nose. I can handle that! This makes sense! It's not hard! But HOW DO I FIND PEOPLE? Isn't that where I start to sound "salesy"?

You're waiting for the "salesy" pitch to kick in. I'm telling you, there's no part that's "salesy" for me. Ever since I have started this business it has been about education. It's about loving people more than my fear. It's about meeting people in that place they channel deep inside, to protect their kids and home. No momma ever said, "I can't wait to poison my family with blue dye in my dish soap today." The thing is... they're not even aware of the poison. You have to start from that place with them and connect in that desire to protect their homes. If you find that connection, you have unlocked the entire secret to Young Living: loving people.

For now, let me give you a few tips just to get you off the ground because that's what this is. It's a getting-started book. It's a show-me-what-I-need-to-do-so-I-can-slay-this-business book. I'm not here to overwhelm you. I'm simply here to equip you. I want to put a few basic tools in your hands so you can see that you are capable, able, and amazing—and you CAN do a Young Living business.

This chapter is tough to write. This is the one place where everyone gets stuck. If they are going to drop the business, it's because of this one thing. They cannot get people to listen. Most people quit network marketing by the 11th month of their business because they cannot get people to class.

Here's the thing... people will listen to you for two reasons: your passion and your compassion. You must have passion for toxic-free living and for Young Living. You need to believe in the products. You must have compassion to listen to people, hear their needs, and meet them in that space. Let me walk you through what that looks like. If you can master this one thing, you really have 100% market share. Every single person you see, whether it be on the street or in casual conversation could end up on your team. The thing that holds you back is fear, not a lack of an audience. If I can untrain fear out of you, the world is at your fingertips.

Here is my simple formula for connecting with people that I do not know (or even those that I do know):

- ♟ Ask leading questions.

- ♟ Find common ground.

- ♟ Respond to questions with questions.

- ♟ Stop talking for two minutes and listen.

- ♟ Meet them in their place of need.

All of that = starter kit

Let me walk you through this step by step. Start by asking leading questions. If you're in the grocery store, it would go something like this: "Your kids are so cute! You have two? I am a mom and by now, my kids would be tossing toilet paper at one another."

Here's a few more examples of leading questions: "Wow, you're great at..." "What do you do for a living?" "You look stressed! Are you ok?"

I once sold a starter kit because of an oversized bag of popcorn. I'm not kidding! I have a heart for missionaries; and I had gone to Alaska to speak to a mission's team that works with Athabascan Indians. I found out that they really liked Pure Protein Complete (that's an AMAZING protein powder that I use for my kids every morning for smoothies instead of sugary cereal). This family did not have a blender and could not afford one. I went to Sam's Club to pick one up and leave it with them without them knowing. Unfortunately, as I walked in the store (about two hours away), the family WALKED RIGHT IN as I was in the check-out line! Apparently, it was the only Sam's within driving distance! I grabbed a bag of popcorn on an end cap nearby that was about the third of my body and leaned on it while I talked with them to hide the blender that was on the conveyor belt behind me. After they walked away, I realized the cashier had been waiting a good 60 seconds for me to stop talking. In my check-out flurry I ended up leaving with the popcorn in my hands... *and* the blender. The blender was sent with the person dropping me off at the airport, and then back to the missionary family. The popcorn, however, ended up with me on the airplane as its own carry on because it was so large.

I sat down in my seat and a woman sat down next to me with a full glottal laugh that filled the plane. She said "What are you doing with that popcorn on your lap?? It's as tall as you!" I said, "I like popcorn?" That kicked off a five-hour overnight conversation that led to why I was in Alaska, why I was teaching classes, toxic-free living, and eventually four starter kits for the woman and her three adult kids.

Meet people where they are.

For her, toxic-free living was on the brain. However, we needed the connection of the popcorn (my leading question) to open the dialogue. After that, it was smooth sailing- because we both like to protect our kids. That's finding common ground.

The most important thing, though, is listening. If you are quiet for two minutes, most people will tell you more than you ever needed to know about themselves. Ask a leading question and stand down. Listen to them. Offer an oil out of the starter kit for their needs. Meet them in their place of frustration, in their place of need. All of that equals a starter kit.

Where do I find people?

When you open your front door, you see... humans. Talk to the humans. It may be someone you see regularly on your daily walk. It may be someone you connect with at the SPCA taking care of abandoned animals. It may be a parent who sat next to you on the sidelines of a basketball court as you watch your kids play who has a nasty cough. It may be the woman walking down the aisle in front of you at church with a cane who needs pain relief. The trick is to keep your eyes open for needs. They are all around you. You will see them every single day if you start to look. Then offer a offer a sample of an oil that could help, or a class on CD (Such as: the 101 class or Toxin Free Life class). Collect their contact information (friend them on Facebook or Instagram), touch base in follow up.

What if they don't respond? The thing is, you're providing something that they need. The parent at the game needs a Thieves cough drop. The woman in church needs Cool Azul Pain cream. They need toxin free living. They haven't connected their hurt, pain, exhaustion or fatigue with lifestyle decisions. You are the one that carries that message. Show love for them, meet them in that place, and tell you have something that may help them with their struggles. Most people will not walk away if you have a solution to their problem. They walk away if you're trying to sell them something.

Here's the cardinal rule: don't walk up to someone and say "Hi! I'm Sarah Harnisch! Would you like to buy my starter kit?" They'll run away screaming. The same holds true if you're connecting with someone you haven't talked with in 10 years on Facebook. You can't strike up a conversation, ask them about their kids, and then in sentence two say that you're launching a Young Living business and ask that they come to a class. That doesn't fly. People can spot that a mile away. Look for needs, offer suggestions, and meet them in their place of need. That's how to walk away from this without being a salesperson, and without losing friends. It's about education of a toxic-free lifestyle, and offering healthy solutions to struggles, not "sales." You become a world-changer. The wisdom and knowledge that you have (even if it's only from the two scripts in the back of this book) will change lives.

Where are some other common places you can find people?

Start by making a list of every single person you know. Organize the list in spots such as: the *Gameplanner* or in the *Gameplan workbook* (two other books I've written at oilabilityteam.com). Carry it with you for 30 days; and write down every face you see: the man at the gas station every single morning, the teacher at your son's school that has expressed an interest in natural products, and the people in your small group at church. Those are the names that go down first. This list is by no means comprehensive, but here are a few more ideas of places you can pull names from:

🧍 Your Facebook friends list

🧍 Your Instagram or Twitter or Snapchat friends list

🧍 Parents of your kid's friends

🧍 Your children's teachers

- ♟ Your address book

- ♟ Your Christmas card list

- ♟ Your wedding invite list

- ♟ Everyone in every cubicle at work

- ♟ The place where you volunteer

- ♟ Faces you see at hobbies you love like the gym, a gardening club, hiking, etc...

- ♟ Parents at your kid's sports games

- ♟ Church, small group, ministry opportunities

- ♟ Your spouse's place of work and contacts list and extended family

- ♟ Your five closest friends' family and friends

- ♟ Faces you see regularly at gas stations, local stores, the post office, spa, hair salon, coffee shops, etc....

Also, check your cell phone. An MIT study in 2015 found the average person had 315 contacts in their cell phone, and talked with a staggering 47 contacts regularly. It only takes a team of about 100 to get to Silver, and the average Silver income is $2088 a month, according to the 2017 Young Living Income Disclosure Guide! With only one in three people on your cell phone contacts list, you could build a viable business. See the MIT study here: http://web.mit.edu/bentley/www/papers/phonebook-CHI15.pdf

There are so many places to pull from! That does not account for your cold market. "Cold" and "Warm" are network marketing terms for the people you don't know (cold) and the people you do know (warm). If you become comfortable in talking to people you have just met, opporunities are endless.

Don't Be Afraid of the No's

We tend to take the word "no" as a personal rejection, or a reflection on our personal character. The two are actually not related. Rejection is completely the opposite of how marketing works. The more "no's" you receive in this, the more you're working your business. "NO" now does not mean "NO" forever. One of the Gold leaders on my team was cleaning a bathroom with a good friend of hers. It was a friend she'd approached a few times about a starter kit that "didn't have the money." The conversation turned to toothpaste. She said, "Why don't we get your kit right now, and I can help you navigate the website; and we'll add toothpaste to your order?" The woman ordered a kit on the spot, added toothpaste; and set up her Essential Rewards. The first several conversations led to no fruit. However, with gentle persistence, she ended up on the leader's team.

Most people don't understand that when they sign up they become part of a business family. They say "no" for a variety of reasons. It's almost never a statement on their relationship with you. You need to be accepting of the "no's". The more "no's" you get, the closer you are to the "yes's". Having zero "no's" means you're not sharing. Studies show that the average person can only say no seven times. That doesn't mean you should pester them. It does mean you're forever networking, and always looking for open spaces to have short conversations on what oils have done in your life. That's seed planting; and it's how you build your business.

One of the most valuable tools I've used to build short conversations is the Marco Polo app on my cell phone. Shooting a tiny 10 second video through the app allows me to say a lot more than texting 25 times to convey my message. Start by downloading Marco Polo and messaging a few friends to join. Have casual conversations with them that do not include the topic of oils. Always invest in people. If they say no, it doesn't mean you're bad at this. It's exactly the opposite: you're working it. Standard network marketing numbers across every company in the United States show that three in every four people will say no (but not necessarily forever). Here's the cool part of the story: one in four "yes's" is enough to build to Royal Crown Diamond, if you do not give up.

Here's a sentence you need to learn: "I want to be your person." When you get to the part of the conversation where you hone-in on how to order a kit, you tend to feel bad that they are spending money. Simply learn language to make sure you do not shy away from the sale. Slip into your training so that it doesn't feel awkward. Don't start the conversation by saying "do you know anyone doing oils? Then you should talk to them." The person they know either isn't doing the business or has poor follow up if they are not

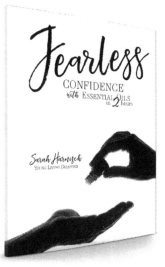

already signed. If the Lord has placed them in your network, simply say "I want to be your person. I want to be there alongside you to train you how to use oils. I want to walk this with you. This is my referral link. When you order, you bless my family. You are now part of a powerful network of oilers. We will help you get started. We will get you plugged in. It's simple. It's easy. And it will totally change how you care for your family."

You are their *person*. That's where this starts.

Here's the thing: every day, you have to be out there selling you. They buy the kit because they feel you care about them. Build relationships without the oils; and that will lead to conversations about the oils. Share who you are. Then stand back and listen, and build relationships. Be real, raw, and genuine. Invest in people. Collect "no's". Keep moving. People give up on network marketing far too soon. Go into it expecting no's and keep your feet in forward motion. You will be blown away as those no's, one by one, slowly join your team in the future. It shows that your fire is unstoppable when you continue to move forward and each yes will energize and ignite you!

Let's move to the next topic to get your business off the ground: the power of the close.

Chapter 4

Don't Shy Away from the Close

What is a "close?" A close is how you end your class. It adds power and strength to your teaching. Outside of telling your personal story and getting oils in their nose, it's one of the most important parts of what you do. It's passion. Let me give you an example.

You could end your class like this: "You've survived Essential Oils 101!! Thank you for coming to my class. I'll teach another class next month. I hope you can come"

Another option is to end a class like this: "Young Living has completely changed my life. Every single aspect of my home is different: how I care for my kids; what tools I use to support their little bodies; and even what products I use in the bathroom. I am not going to be one of the statistics. I choose to fight back. I will not leave my home unguarded. It's so important that you look with a critical eye at the products in your cabinets. The way I do that is with a Young Living starter kit. That's what started this whole journey for me. I'm committed to coming alongside you and helping you get every drop out of that kit, to train you in a safer way. This is something you NEED to take seriously. I have a laptop at the back of the room set up to help you navigate the website. When you walk out this door, you'll have education in your hands to get you started right. Let's do this together."

Do you see the power of a close? The first example was a leader on my team who had had 20 classes with an average class size of 24 people; and she did not sell a single kit. I sat through her class and questioned someone who was leaving. That person told me they had no idea she was doing the business. They would have purchased under her, but she never offered it. Therefore, they found someone else instead.

Why do we shy away from closing? This is the part of Young Living that feels "salesy" to us. We don't want to pitch sales to our friends.

Hear my heart here. You are offering them something they cannot find anywhere else. There is no other company on earth doing what Young Living is doing. Attempts to copy our distillation methods (developed by founder, Gary Young) have been world-wide. There is no Seed to Seal promise of purity anywhere else. There are no farms that you can go visit if you choose. We're a pioneer. We were the first to offer Over the Counter Medications infused with oils; and the very first (globally) to have government approval for Acne Treatment; Cool Azul Pain Cream; and Thieves Cough drops. Young Living's oils distilled at the perfect tempera-ture to best preserve the constituents that enact change in the human body. Therefore, it still maintains the therapeutic benefits, harvested at its peak, grown without toxic weed killers, pesticides, fertilizer, and grown without genetically modified seeds. It run through eight-point testing in triplicate at the farm, at the bottling facility in Spanish Fork, Utah, and again after it's packaged. Young Living has nearly two-billion dollars in sales annually as of 2019, with 600 life-changing products, 16 corporate partners and independent labs, six million global members, 20 international markets, and 50 highly trained scientists running testing for purity. 90-percent of them were hand-trained by Gary Young himself. What does that mean? It means the products work and people keep coming back. It means it's a name you can trust. No other company with hundreds of oils has been around for over 25 years. Our library of how to distill and properties of plans is unequalled globally. If you want to know more about why Young Living is the best, I shot an interview with Young Living's Global Supply Manager, Lauren Walker, called, "Seed to Seal Simplified" that is very powerful. Check it our for free and share it with your teams by visiting oilabilityteam.com. It means Young Living has integrity and it's different than anything else you can get out there. It is the best of the best of the best. And it's safe for you to share it with your friends.

You need to experience that feeling of walking into your best friend's home and seeing Thieves hand soap on their bathroom counter. There is a peace in knowing their family is protected. There is a freedom in knowing you have the same values when it comes to safe-guarding your home. You WANT that in your mom's home and friends' homes. You don't want them exposed to toxic chemicals. Share it. Share it from a place of security knowing you are training them on things that are good, and that will make a sweeping difference in their lives. That will change how they view every single product they use forever; and in a good way. You're not costing them money. You're saving them from poison. And THAT is worth talking about. You will never walk into a friend's home, see Thieves and think, "I said someting to them!" You will think, "I have protected them from poison and taught them a better way. They are safe and tht is peace!"

It goes back to the concept of education over sales. Focus on keeping them informed.

Still not comfortable closing? Then practice. A lot of the time, if I have the words on my tongue already, they roll out of my mouth inadvertently, as if I have skill! Go to the back of this book and read through the close several times until it feels comfortable to you. Then attach it to the 101 or 102 class. Your family and your friends are worth fighting for. Don't be "salesy". Be bold. Be authentic. Be genuine. Be real. If you speak from a place of passion and warmness, people will usually listen to what you have to say. It doesn't make logical sense to clean your home with poisons. If they don't grasp oils, start with Thieves. That's why I gave you two scripts at the end of this mini book. But however you speak to their heart, speak from a place of brokenness at your journey. Be real and connect. That's how you reach someone—not with canned responses and memorized lines, but with a deep passion for what Young Living has done for you. Authenticity is the key to a close. Speak to their heart, speak to the protection of their family, don't give lists of facts. If you skip the head knowledge and speak to that place inside them that longs to protect those closest to them, you're speaking to a deep place that they will remember long after the class.

CHAPTER 5

THE "NUTS AND BOLTS" OF ESSENTIAL REWARDS

What is Essential Rewards? Is this another thing Young Living is trying to get me to buy?? Absolutely not. Here's the thing... you *MUST use* the products to *teach* the products. If you've not placed an order except for your starter kit, how do you train the lifestyle? If you order the same two or three products each month, like Thieves cleaner and laundry soap, you have no starting point to connect to the momma who needs to understand the benefits of Pure Protein Complete to get her kids off sugary cereal in the morning. You ned to live the lifestyle to share it. It's cliché, but you must be a product of the product. I have added countless people to my organization just by wearing oils or having a diffuser going near me. It works.

It all starts by getting the products in your home. That's what Essential Rewards is all about.

Essential rewards is an auto-ship program. There... I said it. I don't like to say it like that in my classes, because words matter. I actually tell it like this: "It's like Christmas every MONTH at your doorstep!" Because it truly is. You get to discover more than 200 single oils and blends. Plus you'll swap out the "yuck" from your cabinets each month, knowing the stuff you *were* using is NEVER coming back. I don't like to give you a line-by-line system for swapping things out. I believe the Lord will lay on your heart where it's most important for you to begin, whether it's your bathroom or your cleaning supplies cabinet. I did put together a neat tool to get you started based on your convictions. It's a tool that's sold over a million copies and went to number one on Amazon. It's called *Fearless*.

My advice to you is that *Fearless* is the second book you read after this. At the end of the book, are 10 challenges. It's everything I want you to know about oiling in your first thirty days, such as: how to log into the Virtual Office and reorder; getting your diffuser going each day (it only takes twenty-one days to form a habit!); the facts and science behind oiling; how to create your own blends and play with that kit on your shelf, how to engage in the Simple Swap (where you go room by room, and cabinet by cabinet cleaning out each space of toxic "yuck", and how to label read, research, and look for poisons in your home. I even designed a *free* calendar (at oilabilityteam.com) that you can use as a checklist as you learn to oil. The calendar gives suggestions, room by room for products to kick out (and what Young Living products to replace it with). Take the challenge yourself, then run your growing team through it each time a new member gets a kit. *Fearless* is the first thing I put in their hands, with their *Fearless* calendar. And it works!

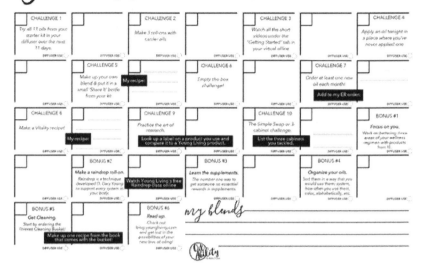

One of the things I love about training your team to research is that they get really good at finding dangers in the home and swapping things out. Point them to reference guides like the ones found on Life Science Publishing (discoverlsp.com). Add them to the EOC on Facebook (the "Essential Oils Club" with Crown Diamond Jim Bob Haggerton for product education). Jim Bob Haggerton is a chiropractor who is incredibly knowledgeable on product. Then of course, there is always Google! Tell them to type in what they are looking for, then "Young Living". Doing a "Young Living pain relief" search will yield Cool Azul pain cream. Train your team to look things up for themselves and be self-sufficient so you're not answering questions at two in the morning.

What did my personal Essential Rewards journey look like? Once I saw what oils could do, I knew I wanted #alltheoils. I got a reference guide, and looked up the uses of many of the oils. I even wrote my family's names next to each oil in the catalogue that came with my kit. You learn by playing, and by looking things up, not by being an expert. I was not an aromatherapist when I got my kit. I am not a doctor. I'll never be able to diagnose. However, I know enough to research. Any mom or dad can open a guide and look up "ear" or "knee" and find oils that can help. Once I knew what several oil or oil-infused products were known for, I made an Essential Rewards wish list based on order of importance. It went something like this:

- **Month 1:** NingXia Essential Rewards + oils for the top three things I wanted to work on in my wellness journey

    I also included a few supplements for each member of my family. Our "core four" (the four supplements all seven of us take without fail) are: NingXia, Omegagize, Essentialzyme-4, and Life 9.

- **Month 2:** Thieves Essential Rewards bundle + Thieves laundry soap

- **Month 3:** Golden Touch Kit (I wanted to double my oils collection as swiftly and as affordably as I could)

- **Month 4:** Raindrop kit: Everyone NEEDS this kit. Go to https://www.youngliving.com/raindrop/ to learn how to use it.

- **Month 5:** Simple Swap: I went room by room according to the Fearless book and started kicking toxins out by room. First, I tackled my cleaning cabinets. Then, I took on the challenge of my kitchen and laundry room.

- **Month 6:** Personal care: I pampered myself after six months on Essential Rewards and ordered the ART Cleansing trio; and I also started some face pampering. Then, I morphed into Savvy makeup, and all the personal care products like Thieves Dentarome toothpaste and Copaiba Vanilla shampoo. I've never looked back.

If you need some conviction, a tangible reason to go all-natural, a great resource to understand the science of the dangers in your home is Doctor Olivier Wenker's book, "A Doctor's Guide to Essential Rewards." He does a fantastic job of providing evidence-based research on the "why" behind oiling. Doctor Oli was Young Living founder, Gary Young's, personal physician and trusted friend. He's a walking encyclopedia of knowledge; and his scientific background will WOW you on the dangers in your home.

The path to cleaning out your own home will look much different than mine. There are many ways to get from point A to point B in building your oils arsenal, and no particular way is incorrect. Start in the place where you feel most convicted. Start small; and don't get overwhelmed. It's a journey in that we're constantly learning from each other, we're constantly reading new literature and focusing on science research information that comes out each year. I was sitting in a class last night and learned new uses of Helichrysum from a Star member on my team. She gave me tips I'd never heard of before. Knowledge isn't dictated by rank or by the number of degrees or certifications you have. It's dictated by experience, playing with the oils and looking things up. You'll never get to a place where you know it all. The Lord made something amazing when He created the plants! It may take a lifetime to learn them, but I'm in it for the long haul. I have never missed the toxins in my home.

Protection Over Perfection

Your home may not be perfect; but perfection is not the goal. Protection is the goal. With each chemical you kick to the curb, it's one less toxin you need to protect your family from. Look at progress, not the work ahead. Then train that passion of protection into your growing team. That is how you blow up your business! Building it one brick at a time, one story at a time, one oil that shows up on an Essential Rewards order that you never knew existed, one passage in a desk reference, or one conversation with an oiler. Oils are studied piece by piece and brick by brick. And then you look out over the people you have impacted; and you're sitting atop an oils empire simply because of your passion for helping others.

Let's dig deeper into the language of Young Living so I can guide you on some terminology. Learn the lingo so you can train the lifestyle.

Let me go over a couple network marketing words. It truly is like learning a whole new language when you first start learning.

PV: Personal volume. This is the volume of products purchased (by you) in a month. It can include orders on Quick Order or Essential Rewards. Note: Quick Orders do not allow you to accrue Essential Rewards points; but you can 'cash in' on your Essential Rewards points with this button.

PGV: Personal group volume. This is the volume outside your qualifying legs.

OGV: Organization group volume. This is what you purchase each month, and the sales of the entire organization under you. It resets to "0" on the first day of the next month.

Leg: Is a person and the team under them.

Upline: These are the people "above" you in your organization. Likewise, the "downline" are the people below you.

Enroller: The person responsible for introducing a new distributor to Young Living.

Sponsor: A new distributor's direct upline and main support. The sponsor may also be the enroller. This is where a new oiler is "placed" on your team.

Essential Rewards: An autoship program to build your oils arsenal cost effectively.

Essential Rewards are Young Living products you pick out every month (either the same products that you love, or new products you want to try). You can tweak it every month, or last month's order will ship to you automatically. You need to spend 100PV (PV stands for personal volume) to get your full paycheck. You can think of PV as the value of the product. It doesn't always reflect what the cost is; but for most of the oils, it is dollar for dollar.

Some are floored when I tell them you need to purchase product to be paid. They say, "Is Young Living trying to get something from me?" "No, they are trying to *give* something to you." You can't talk about something you've never tried. You can't have passion for the products when there are no products. If they were trying to get something from you, you'd see the amount you must spend go up every single time you rank up. But whether you are a Star or a Royal Crown Diamond, it never changes. It's always 100PV to get paid. Make sure your order each month is above that number; or you may be missing out on all the hard work you did that month teaching classes and building your team.

What does Essential Rewards mean for your business? Everything! It is the cornerstone of all you do. There is no rank up without Essential Rewards. After a year, if your new oiler has purchased the kit and nothing after that first order, they will drop off your team. If your goal is to hit rank after rank, and grow a willable income, it's dependent on people understanding the lifestyle and making swaps in their home. Otherwise, what you do is for naught. That is the message that must be trained. It's hard to rank to Star (the first rank) or Senior Star (the second rank) if every class you teach, you start right back over at 0PV the following month. Essential Rewards is the first brick. You stand on it the next month to continue laying the foundation of your business.

There is no Young Living business without Essential Rewards. You can sign 50 people on your team, but if you never train the lifestyle, in a year they are likely to drop off as if they were never there to begin with. Not getting your team on board with Essential

Rewards is like working 20 days this month, then coming in next month and it's as if all 20 days never happened. Your work never existed. That's what happens when you lay the groundwork when signing people with kits; but never follow through with teaching the lifestyle. 0's on your team (due to those not ordering) = no rank up.

THE POWER OF ER

You understand ER is critical for ranking up; and you have a plan for your own personal orders... however, logistically, how does it work? Let's tackle 30 seconds of network marketing math. If you were to teach four classes next month, and one person at each class got a kit, you would have a PV of 400 at the end of the month, (not including your order). Once you place your monthly order, you would rank to Star, which requires a minimum PV of 500. If the next month, none of them are on Essential Rewards, you start right back over at 0. The rank is gone, and you have to do all the work a second time. But if the next month two of them got on ER—one at 300PV and one at 100PV, with your order, you're at Star before you even start the month.

The second month, when you teach four classes, and four more people sign up, or maybe five people this month, you're running for your second rank and an income of $235 a month (according to the Income Disclosure Guide). A Star ranking is then in your rearview mirror. Essential Rewards is the soul of your business. It's what keeps it alive. It's how you achieve each rank. It's lifestyle training instead of starter kit training. Don't train the starter kit, train the lifestyle. That's how you rock this thing!

Your new oiler must spend 50PV in **a year** to keep their account active. That's the equivalent of a bottle of Thieves cleaner and a Thieves laundry soap to stay active in a calendar year. There are no yearly membership dues and no fees to pay to be part of Young Living; only a desire to kick chemicals to the curb.

One amazing blessing that Young Living did in 2018 was make it possible for your new oiler to join Essential Rewards AT SIGNUP. This is HUGE; because it means that their starter kit (worth 100PV)—can count toward Essential Rewards points. Immediately on your first Essential Rewards order, you get 10% back. After four consecutive months on Essential Rewards, it's 20% back. After 25 months, it's 25% back. That's like going into the grocery store, and EVERY SINGLE TIME you buy laundry soap forever you get 25% back!

On top of that, if you hit certain tiers of PV, Young Living gifts additional oils and products you may have never used before. It's the fastest way to build your oils collection. They usually offer freebies for 190PV, 250PV, 300PV, and sometimes even 400PV. One month, the 300PV tier was worth more than 200PV. That's like saying, "give me 300 dollars, and I'll hand you 200 dollars right back." When you factor in the Essential Rewards points you've earned on top of that (30 points in the first three months, 60 points on month four, and 75 points on month 25), it is, by far, the most affordable way to build your collection and swap toxic chemicals. Let's look at actual examples of how this works. I grabbed a few previous months of Young Living's giveaways for hitting certain tiers on Essential Rewards. In one example, I spent $300 and got $216 back just by stocking my laundry soap, dish soap, and other products i loved and needed. No doubt this is a GREAT call. Essential Rewards is the Young Living version of extreme couponing; except everything on your order is something pure that you actually want in your home. Here is what it looks like on paper.

These are actual promos Young Living offered in 2019:

- **Sample month 1:** 300PV: Freebies at this tier include: Thieves Household cleaner, Kunzea oil, Thieves foaming hand soap, Thieves fruit and veggie soak, Thieves dish soap, Orange Vitality oil. Retail value $186.05. (Spend 300, get $30 back in points and $186 of free product.)

- **Sample month 2:** 400PV: Freebies at this tier include: 15ml Ylang Ylang oil, 5ml Purification oil, 5mL Palo Santo oil, 15ml Cypress oil, Super Cal Plus Supplement, 5ml Clove oil, 5ml Marjoram oil. (3 of these oils are part of the 9 used in the Raindrop Technique!) Retail value: $212.83. Spend 400 stocking products you need for your home, get $40 back in points and $212.83 in free product.)

- **Sample month 3:** 300PV: Freebies at this tier include: 5ml PanAway oil, 15ml Longevity oil, Life 9 Supplement, 15ml Citrus Fresh oil, 5ml Digize Vitality oil. Restock your personal cleaning supplies and care products for your home at 300PV (products you'd already order); but you'd also get $30 in points and $174.02 in free product. That's $204 free for spending $300.

This is why Essential Rewards is amazing. It's how you double and triple your oils collection, learn about the product by playing with it and looking it up, and be a passionate product of the product so others fall in love to0.

If you're not a numbers person but need something visual, check out the value of what I just said in the charts below. They only calculate Essential Rewards points, not the free oils you get every single month as well. I'm completely fine accruing points and getting my laundry soap, hand soap, and toothpaste for free! They're products I buy and use every month anyway. If I can get it by stocking oils and Young Living products in my home, it's actually saving me in my monthly budget.

the value of
ESSENTIAL REWARDS

	3 MONTHS	6 MONTHS	12 MONTHS	2 YEARS	5 YEARS
50PV	$15	$45	$105	$225	$765
100PV	$75	$165	$345	$705	$2,325
190PV	$312	$681	$1,419	$2,625	$7,665
250PV	$495	$1,065	$2,205	$4,485	$14,995
300PV	$690	$1,470	$3,030	$6,150	$16,050

BASED ON POINTS EARNED PLUS ESTIMATED VALUE OF MONTHLY PROMOTIONS

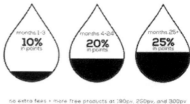

ESSENTIAL

YOUR OILS. YOUR WAY. EVERY MONTH.

| months 1-3 **10%** in points | months 4-24 **20%** in points | months 25+ **25%** in points |

no extra fees + more free products at 190pv, 250pv, and 300pv

REWARDS

Let me add one more thing here. Whatever freebies Young Living is offering each month (you can view them on the front page of your Virtual Office), I always like to order at least up to the highest tier. If 300PV is the offering for free oils that month, I will order 300PV. If it's 400PV, I will order 400. Why? Because it gives me more opportunity to learn about new oils (that I get for free!); and I get more ER points to use for my home. The more you know, the more you share. It's an investment in your business that pays out in your grocery budget, and in your knowledge base as you continue to learn and grow more each month and fall more and more in love with Young Living.

It's taken me four years, but I've now swapped out all of my toxic cleaning supplies for everything Young Living. I swapped my cereal routine for Pure Protein complete, my personal care products for Young Living like deodorant, shampoo, and Mirah hair oil (bye bye split ends!), and my supplements switched for Young Living's supplements. I've never looked back. After nearly five years into this journey, according to the chart above, I've saved nearly $16,000 dollars. That's a lot of dish soap I didn't have to pay for! My oils racks are well stocked as well!

Atop of that, there is now YL Go, which is the Amazon Prime of Young Living and YL Go is $59 for the basic package. It's $129 yearly for YL Go Plus and your shipping is free. YL Go is 13 months of free shipping. YL Go+ gives you an extra 24 flex shipment credits that you can use if you run out of toothpaste in the middle of the month.

Other perks to Essential Rewards: You choose the date it ships; you customize your order to what you want and need for your home and family each month, Essential Rewards shipping rates are discounted beyond regular orders; you accrue free oils at each of the PV tiers; and earn a rare oils blend called "Loyalty". The "Loyalty" oil was designed by Gary Young before he passed away. You receive these perks after being on Essential Rewards for 12 consecutive months. It was his thank you to members for their love of Young Living.

Following Up

How often do I follow up, and how do I follow up? Isn't it awkward talking to a person a second time if they have not yet gotten the kit? Aren't I being pushy?? No. This is a different topic than collecting no's that we discussed in Chapter 3. For that, it's initial contact. Following up is what you do after you make contact with someone and they did not get a kit. It's the second conversation. It can feel awkward, but it's a huge skill you need for your business.

It took the woman that signed me SEVEN weeks to get my attention. I attended the class. She wrote me the next week. I said I had interest in the kit, but not yet. She wrote me in week two; and I gave the same answer. The same action was repeated in weeks three, four, five, six, and seven. Shown in studies, the average person can only say no seven times. I perfectly align with those averages; because on June 27th 2014, I got my kit. I immediately fell in love after I started playing with it. Then on July 18th I taught my first class. I had no idea that there was such freedom on the other side of the starter kit! If I'd only known then what I know now, and how much our lives would change!

If you go into every conversation leading with the person and their needs; and if you are checking in, you're not pushy or "salesy". If you're uncomfortable picking up the phone, remember that you're there to serve them. If it's someone you've never met before, simply ask them in the initial conversation if you can "Facebook friend" them. There's enough distance there for them to feel safe (they can always unfriend you if they thought you were strange!) You now have their contact information in a way that doesn't give out your personal address or phone number. Then you simply carry on the conversation the way you would if you were checking on a friend. For example "Hey, you seemed pretty stressed today! I am just checking in to see if your work day got better. I worked in retail for several years, and I remember how rough it was on me. That little oils book I gave you changed my life. I'll write you in a couple days to see if you were able to check it out. I believe it's the answer for what you're looking for." Always keep it about them, and never about you, sales, or your business. That's solid follow up.

Now let me flip this upside down on you. How MANY times do you pursue someone that keeps telling you they have an interest in the kit; but never move forward? I give it three shots. I make contact three times. I hand out a sample only once. After that, they're taking advantage of you. After three tries, I will continue building the relationship and seed dropping; but if they aren't picking up the lifestyle, it's not the right time. It will drain you and damage your relationship. Move on. Stay in contact, but focus on fresh faces.

What about following up for those that already have a kit, but are not on Essential Rewards? I love to use these lines: "Hey, you invested in yourself by getting this kit. I want to help you get every drop out of your investment! You have joined a powerful oils education team, and we want to come alongside you and train you how to use these amazing oils. What's the best way of reaching you—texting or email?" Just start the conversation. As they express interest, you can find out what their greatest needs are and target resources directly to them so they have a reason to get on Essential Rewards. Don't give a way out to say no. Give them options where both answers are "yes". These leading sentences work really well, too, for people you did not personally sign that are on your team.

Ideas for lead-in sentences to kick off a follow up conversation:

- "How are you doing? I was checking in on you after..."

- "Tell me your favorite thing about the textable class!"

- "What are your biggest health struggles right now? I don't feel like we had a good chance to talk earlier."

- "I am touching base! I have not had a chance to connect with you in the last few days. You seemed pretty down last time we talked. How are you feeling?"

Here are a few sentences I will NOT use:

- "Have you listened to the 101 cd I gave you in the purple bag yet???"

- "Why haven't you responded to my calls about hosting a class?"

- "You said you wanted a kit, but I've waited three weeks and you're still not on my team. Is something wrong?"

In the first few sentences, I led with them. In the last few, you're leading with your emotions and your investment in them. Leading with you is never the way to go. Strong follow up always centers around their thoughts, needs, feelings, struggles, and desires. If you start from that place, you'll become a follow up master. Ask a strong leading question that requires a personal response, then it opens a door to speak about oils.

CHAPTER 6

MUST-HAVE TIPS FOR CLASS DAY

I told you earlier that teaching a class is as simple as a kit and script; but there are a few do's and don'ts that will give you a leg up. 80% of your business is simply being prepared.

Do:

♟ Have a clipboard on hand and collect their contact information. Tell them it's so you can pass along oily information later. It's really important they not leave the room without you having a way to touch base (especially if they did not get a kit). Ask if they are interested in you teaching their friends and family about oils.

♟ Have a laptop or computer in the back of the room **with internet access** so they can sign up on the spot. Make sure it's ready to go before you start the class.

♟ Have the starter kit on hand, with the caps off, and ready to pass around. Have a diffuser running.

♟ Have the Essential Rewards promos for that month on display for them to see.

♟ Have purple bags on hand. I put a little organza bag together with *Fearless*, which has instructions on how to order (free on my website on the purple bags page). I include the *Gameplan* mini for those considering the business (it's different from this little book). It's a prospecting book. It's written for someone with no introduction to a Young Living business. It's one dollar. The *Gameplan mini* gives the why behind the business and gets them thinking about it. I also include the book, the *Ignite mini*, which will train you in one afternoon how to do the business. I give a class that they didn't get on cd (if you teach the 101, give those 102: Toxin Free Life, on Thieves, and vice versa). This keeps them interested and coming back. I put a photo of the starter kit in the bag (you can get these for pennies at discoverlsp.com). I do a cover sheet (the ones on my website, which are free printables, say, "You have just been the recipient of the famous purple bag! Here's what's inside!"). I always include a business card so they have a way to get back to me. For instructions on assembling purple bags, visit this site: https://oilabilityteam.com/follow-up-bags/

I will say if you are just starting the business, take your check, and put it in your gas tank. The most important thing for you to be doing is sharing oils. It's more important than any other invest-ment in your business.

DO NOT:

♟ Teach classes sporadically (this is your paycheck! I teach 4-6 classes a month, even as a Diamond)

♟ Get distracted.

♟ Put a lot of time and effort into things that can't be copied by your leaders. The most powerful tool you have is duplication on your team. If you teach a class on a Saturday, you've reached the people in that one class. If you have five leaders out there doing the same action, you just taught six classes in the same space. Don't scare them from the business by complicating things. Keep it simple: script, kit, humans.

We don't need to spend a lot of time on leader training, because that's more for the full Gameplan book. But I can give you a couple simple sentences that you can use from the get-go that will help you inadvertently find people who want to do what you do. A careerbuilder.com survey in 2016 found that one in six Americans were actively looking for a job in the next 12 months. There's no reason they can't be on your team. If you have six people in your class, you're likely looking one possible business leader right in the eyes. There's a way to get their attention without hunting them; just like you don't hunt for product users.

Let me explain with a quick story.

Four years after I got my kit, I did a teacher training with 30 leaders on one of my legs. A woman walked in that I recognized from one of my very first classes. She had gone inactive. I assumed she placed a 50PV order and reactivated without my contacting her; but that was not the case. When I approached her, she said, *"Oh! I did not realize I was still on your team! I signed up under my friend because I felt like I could do the business under her. When I saw how much I had to do, in order to do it like you; I realized it was more than I could take on. I did not have the time or the money to do it your way. I did not realize she was under you: and that I am still on your team."*

That was a punch to the gut; but it made me scrutinize every action I did at 101 classes. Am I scaring my leaders away? Can I be copied? Your budding leaders have the most fire at their very first introductory oils class. Leaders don't need to be hunted. They find you because you give them hope; and because they CAN do what you do. They find you because your actions are simple. If your actions are overloaded with information, you'll have a hard time duplicating. Your organization should grow without pushing the business excessively, because oils are simple. Sharing is simple. Freedom is simple. We are the ones that make it complicated. One of my biggest mistakes at the start of my business was overcomplicating things that were quite simple.

I didn't start leading with the business until I was nearly a Diamond status and deeply wanted the income for every person I met. I fell in love with freedom even more than oils. It was a process; and it wasn't something I felt immediately when the starter kit showed up at my door. I hadn't tasted freedom yet. By the time I was a Diamond, I figured if a momma of five from the projects, living in the middle of nowhere, could pull this off, there is no reason everyone I met couldn't do it. I just shared oils passionately; and the leaders came of their own volition. They came because they needed hope. They needed income. They needed purpose.

Stop looking for leaders. Simply end each class by saying, "Would you like to learn how to get your oils for free? The little book *Your Gameplan: Build A Life Beyond Survival Mode* is in your purple bag. Read it; and I'll touch base with you in two days." That is the extent of my business training in 101 classes. And yet with those 3 sentences, I picked up over 800 leaders the first two years of my business. Keep your language and your actions simple.

What kind of actions scare your leaders away?

♟ Putting a lot of money into food at your classes (i.e. Peppermint Vitality brownies).

♟ Having a large spread of aromatherapy books on the table that they can't afford.

♟ Having folders of photocopied information on oils for each person.

♟ Creating a poster board with all the oils stories you've collected.

♟ Showing off all Young Living products ever created at an intro class. Do they need to know about Seedlings in a 101 class? There's no Seedlings Starter kit (so I'd say no). It's information overload. New builders won't have those resources. They have a script, a kit, and people.

♟ Getting a Cricut cutter and decorating all your bottles with pretty word stickers.

♟ Going for an aromatherapy certification and being "the expert". The less you know, the more you can be copied. Train people to look things up. Don't be the know it all. Say things like, "I'm not sure about that. I just looked up 'ear' in my reference guide!"

♟ Doing pricey make and takes with supplies that must be pur chased from multiple websites that are not from the Young Living Virtual Office. (Corporate said 70 percent of people that attend make and take classes never order the oil and never make the craft again. If you are building a business, that is not the shortest point from A to B.)

♟ Making oily side products "for sale" like oils racks, diffuser necklaces, or hand-sewn oils bags. It is a distraction that is costing time toward earning higher rank. Freedom for your family is on the other side of teaching. Stay focused on growing your team. Oils racks do not lead to "Diamondships". The money is in your downline, not any side business you generate. Save your side businesses for when you hit Royal Crown Diamond and your family is cared for, for life. Every side business you launch is costing your kids freedom. It distracts you for a long enough period of time that you just may think network marketing doesn't work. It does, but you have to do the actions that lead to growth. If you are not teaching classes, training your leaders or training the lifestyle and Essential Rewards, you're not doing actions that lead to rank ups. Side businesses do not grow OGV (Organization Group Volume). And worst of all, leaders will copy you and no one will rank. Do you want your leaders teaching classes or making diffuser neckalces? Be the example.

♟ Doing more than one Multi-Level Marketing business. Hear my heart here! You will be jack of all trades and master of none. You won't rank in either if you try to run two businesses simultaneously. You'll burn yourself out and confuse up and coming leaders who see you posting on two businesses on social media. You are cutting away your ability to duplicate by putting your hands in too many pots.

♟ Selling oily things you have made, like: roll-ons, creams, or "mini starter kits" They won't buy the kit! Also, it's against Policies and Procedures - the rulebook from Young Living! You CANNOT sell samples of Young Living oil in any way. You can review the rules under "Member Resources" in your Virtual Office on the Young Living website. While you are there, also peek at the handful of short videos under the "Getting Started" tab on the front page of your VO to learn more about the incredible company you work for.

♟ Opening a retail storefront with thousands of dollars in oils inventory that must be stocked. Let Young Living do the stocking.

You just be the mouthpiece. Your leaders can't stock a thousand dollars of oils in a store.

Are those things bad? Not necessarily. But save them for a space where you won't scare up-and-coming leaders that don't have the time or resources to do the business the way you are running yours. If you want to gift a roll-on to a leader on your team, go for it. But don't sell it. And save your pretty, decorated bottles for leaders as your organization grows larger, or at #ylunites rallies. A 101 class where you are scouting for new members and business builders to labor beside you is also not the right spot. Always weigh every minute you spend on your business. Is it a distraction, or will it lead to growth? If the answer is it's a distraction, let it go and stay focused. Your goal is freedom. You can rank so much faster if you focus. And your leaders will copy what they see.

CHAPTER 7

WHAT IF THEY DON'T LISTEN TO ME?

(Leak: This is unreleased content from the up-and-coming "Unstuck" book!)

There are actually a lot of reasons why people don't respond; and it's not always because they are saying no to you. They may be legitimately busy. They may be distracted. They may be overwhelmed. They may be amid a major life event. They may not see the value of oils yet. They may not be emotionally or physically in a place to learn something new (even though the desire for clean living is there). There are ten thousand reasons for silence. I wrote in the full *Gameplan* book that you must emotionally detach yourself from the sale of the kit or this business will eat you alive. As stated in Chapter 3, you cannot take every "no", "not yet", or silence as a personal affront. Yet, though we know it in our heads, we still live in a place of fear of rejection. This is why we don't confidently ask people about oils. Without confidence, you are dead in the water. People will only follow what they want for themselves. They will not follow fear.

That's easy to say, but very hard to do. How do I personally get over rejection? It's simple, really. I can answer that question with one word: **volume**. Be so busy sharing with the "next" person, and building the "next" relationship, that you don't have time to notice the "no's". Be so busy teaching classes, handing out purple bags, doing vendor events, or teaching in-person classes. Stay focused on sharing with your warm and cold market, the people you meet and the ones you already know; and love on new faces every single day. You won't have time to tally those that aren't responding. You won't have time to wear the pain of the message that was not responded to, or the hurt of a friend that skipped your class with no explanation. You don't wince at the six people that checked "yes" to come to your event and it was a no-show. Those people aren't even an afterthought to you. That is the evil one messing with your head. You truly won't have time to notice the no's. Just rinse and repeat. Focus on the next person every minute you're running your business. Always look forward, never backward. Backward thinking leads to backward business growth. Your business is in front of you, not behind you. Your freedom is in front of you, not behind you. Run a no-drama team. No-drama starts with you.

If they don't listen to you, what do you do? Kick the dust from your feet and move forward. There are four million distributors globally in Young Living. There are 300 million people in the United States. If every person in the world in Young Living lived in the U.S., in a room of 300 people, just four would have a starter kit. The audience is there. Saturation is a myth. Just stay focused on new faces, even if that means getting outside your comfort zone and opening a conversation with someone you don't know very well. The more "no's" you collect, the harder you are working your business. If you limit your business to your mom, best friend, and cousin, that is amateur network marketing. Look for needs around you. People are everywhere. Oil them up.

FEAR

I need to say something about fear here. There is an innate feeling of inadequacy in just about all of us. There is a fear of rejection. *What will they think of me? Will they think I want to get something from them? Will it ruin my relationship with them? If I don't know them, will they think I am creepy?*

You have GOT to get past that stuff. If your head is asking those questions, you're still stuck in the land of selling. Listen closely: love them more than your fear. They are worth fighting for. If you are meeting a need, there is no reason for them to say no. You are fixing a struggle they have. You are being there for them. That's compassion! Not sales!

I love this sweet note I got from one of my new builders. Whenever I am writing a book, I always test it vigorously on hundreds, sometimes thousands of people. I want to see if it works; and if it gets to the guts of people's questions. Read what she wrote. Maybe this is right where you are:

Megan: *"Fear of rejection is a big issue for me. (I could write a lifetime on this subject). But you nailed it. People have more than once said to me, "I don't want to sell to people". I may have even thought this too! I'm learning though. It really isn't about "selling", but sometimes I think talking too much makes me sound sales"ish". If I just learn to listen, I'm not sounding salesy, I am concerned. If I think I sound salesy, I need to rethink what I am doing. This is where I am in the business. Undoing all I know about sales and learning to educate. There is a huge difference."*

Megan managed 17 department Sears stores and has a background in sales. She knows so much more about selling than I do. But we realized together that she hit the nail on the head. It isn't about selling. My favorite line was "I'm not sounding salesy, I am concerned." Fill a need. That changes the entire game. It's not about your fear or how you are perceived. It's not even if they say yes or no; because that truly doesn't matter. It's how you mentally handle the outcome of the conversation. If you pick yourself up off the ground after each no, you're already focused on the next thing; and that's what leads to rank ups. There are a hundred yes's after the no's. Ultimately, if you can learn to emotionally detach yourself from the response, that's what leads to a Diamondship. "No" now is not "no" forever. "No" now is not a statement on their relationship with you. Move on to those that are ready to listen and ready for change, without emotion or pain.

THE WAIT IS WORTH THE WORK

Another thing I want to plant in your head is the danger of expectation. It's perfectly ok to dream; and even to dream larger than you've ever dreamed in your life. With your hustle and your consistency, those dreams will likely come true. But Young Living is papered with stories of Diamonds that hit Silver in a month or two, Diamond within a year, Royal in two years.... Your road may not be their road. They may have networks you don't have. They may have a platform and a voice you've not built yet. That's ok. It's ok because that is not REQUIRED to get to Diamond. You may not build as fast, but freedom is still freedom. If it takes you 10 years to get paid like a rocket scientist, the wait is worth the work. There are no student loans in network marketing and no business debt that takes 7 years before you see a profit. You love on people, share a script, they order, and Young Living does all the work. Some people do it fast; and some people have more of a cadence to their pace. Both roads lead to Diamond. Don't put an expectation on yourself that if you haven't hit a certain rank in a certain time that "you're just not good at this." That's a lie you're choosing to believe. Pace doesn't matter. Just fight.

CHAPTER 8

STRATEGY: SOMEONE WANTS TO SIGN UP! NOW WHAT??

This is where it starts to get fun. Where do you place people? You nail a strategy system, run with it, and don't deviate from the plan. I'm going to train you on the system Young Living uses; but if your Diamond has trained you otherwise, go with it. They know what they are doing; or they would not have their rank! There are many ways to get from point A to point B. The Rising Star bonus system simply ensures that you get a larger check earlier in your business.

There are only two mistakes you can make when building your organization: build too deep or build too wide. You only need six legs to get to Royal Crown Diamond; so don't build 14 level one legs. You are only paid five levels deep for Unilevel pay; so don't sign someone 12 levels down.

"What the what? What are you talking about?? Sarah!!! You're using network marketing language on me!"

When I talk "deep and wide", I'm explaining where you will sign people. As you start collecting "yes's" at your classes, their kits are the reward as they run for the oils you so passionately trained them on. You met their needs and loved on them in that space without judgement of their lifestyle.

When you first sign someone, they go directly under you. In fact, use that strategy a few more times! Give them your member number (we talked about that in Chapter two); and have them use it as sponsor and enroller when they go to youngliving.com and "become a member" to get their kit. If you can't remember who is who, "e" comes before "s". Enroller is the higher rank. Sponsor is where you place them when you want them on a specific leg to rank or build Rising Star bonuses. Sponsor and enroller simply designates where a person is placed on your team. When you sign up, you become part of a family. You are not just logging onto a website and ordering a product from a store. You're part of something amazing. And where you go matters.

In the same breath, I'll tell you that if you don't like where you are, bloom where you are planted. The Lord makes no mistakes in where you were placed. Don't hunt for other teams to get more "support". Get out there and create your own team culture. Be so busy looking down at your team growing that you don't have time to look up at what you think you don't have. Many, many Diamonds have built without the support of an upline. You have all the tools you need to rock this: a script, a kit, and *YOU*.

Back to strategy.

At the very beginning, everyone goes under you because there is no team yet. With my first class, I had six sign ups. All six went under me as level one's (those are people signed directly under your name. Use your number for both sponsor and enroller). After my next four classes, I had a team of 27 a month later. With a team of 27, some strategy is necessary. A month after that, with consistent teaching, it was 64 people; then 120 in month four. Four years out, there are ten thousand on my team. It's not about me being amazing; it's about the power of a team, and the power of duplication. My goal in this short section is how to train you to get every drop out of your growing paycheck. You do that with solid strategy.

To be a Royal Crown Diamond, you need six legs. (Remember... a leg is a person and a team below them.) Once you are a Silver in Young Living, you get Generation Bonuses. As you are just starting though, for the first few ranks, you can cash in on Rising Star bonuses. Those are cash payouts for having good strategy and laying a foundation for your team that allows you to rank more swiftly. The payouts (called shares) vary each month; but it's usually about 28 to 40 dollars each. You can get several shares for hitting certain strategy benchmarks. For the sake of simplicity, let's call them Step 1, Step 2, and Step 3.

♟ Step 1: is to sign seven people directly under you. Why seven? It gives you a bonus leg if one of your leaders decides to drop off. You have another leg in your back pocket.

Once you have seven signed as your level ones, it's time for some strategy. Each one of those seven has to equal 300PV for it to count as a share. The top of that leg has to spend 100PV for the leg to count. So... say the top spends 100PV, then you sign someone as a level two (they're immediately under your level one); and they spend 200PV... BAM!!! Done!!! That leg is finisimo; and you can move onto the next leg. But wait... the second leg is already consistently spending 300PV. BAM. Done. Move to the third leg. You keep teaching classes and building in a way that you have the base of your business knocked out at the get go. When you're doing advanced strategy, you just take six of those seven legs to Gold; and you have the legs in place to be a Royal Crown Diamond (easy-peasy math). It all works because of duplication.

You have Step 1 nailed. You now have seven legs; and all of them are at 300PV. All your level one's are spending 100PV. You may have some 50PV level two's, or a couple 100PV and 200PV level three's; and that's totally ok. However, the numbers lay out, as soon as all seven are at 300PV. Expect your first Rising Star bonus in your paycheck.

♟ **Step 2:** Take two of those legs to 5000GV. That means when you're teaching classes, you're spinning plates. One class you may place under leg one; and the next, under leg two. You may have four sign ups at a single class and divvying them between the legs so they grow evenly. The goal is to get them to 5000GV at about the same time so you get the Rising Star bonus.

♟ **Step 3:** Take legs one and two and get them to 10000GV. Then take legs three and four and get them to 5000GV. Then you collect all the shares for Rising Star. By this point, you are an Executive in Young Living (the third rank), and well on your way to Silver. You would get a paycheck of more than two-thousand dollars a month. Oh... and your Gold, Platinum, Diamond, Crown Diamond, and Royal Crown Diamond legs have all been started.

One caution with this system: Don't build the legs you don't need yet heavily. That would fall under building too wide. If you need legs one and two at 500 OGV, don't build legs five and six to 500 OGV. You need that volume in the first two legs, so you can get paid. The goal of Rising Star is to lay a foundation, not build all six legs simultaneously. You'll have volume in legs you don't need yet, and will have to wait longer to hit Executive and Silver, because your kit sales are spread out across the six legs, instead of in the first two legs you need to rank up. Build wide enough to get Rising Star, but not so wide that you wait on your next rank. If you stick with the chart below and use those numbers as benchmarks, you'll strategize effortlessly.

Rising Star Method

STEP 3 { 1K 1K 500 500

STEP 2 { 500 500

STEP 1 { 300 300 300 300 300 300 300

I threw a bunch of names at you earlier; so I may as well use this moment to explain what I was talking about. There are nine ranks in Young Living: Star, Senior Star, Executive, Silver, Gold, Platinum, Diamond, Crown Diamond, and Royal Crown Diamond. I'll go through the requirements to hit each rank in Chapter 12.

CHAPTER 9

SAY WHAT? THERE'S MORE THAN ONE WAY TO SHARE?

I've written a whole book on this topic called *Unstuck*. I took two years to compile all the different ways I saw people oiling others up; and complied them into 16 different types of classes. Can't get people to come to class? This may be your answer. Reading a script on a couch to your mom and best friend is only one way of sharing. It may not work for you if it is not your teaching style.

Before I give you synopsis of *Unstuck*, I want to issue one caution. Don't try to share outside of your gift set. For example, we tend to see someone rank quickly by using a skill they already had. (For example: a mom with a large blogging audience). Is a blog a bad way to build? Absolutely not! Several Diamonds also had success. However, if you're not a strong writer, if you have no audience, if you're not tech savvy, if you have no social media marketing skills, and have never heard of WordPress or hosting sites; it's probably not for you. Don't try to learn a new skill to get your business off the ground.

Corporate said at the 2018 Young Living convention that 70 percent of all Young Living businesses are built with in-person classes. 30 percent of businesses are built in all other ways combined, including vendor events, textable classes, Instagram, etc... Does that mean that in person classes are the most successful? Nope! That's not what I'm trying to convey. Many people have built in many ways and have seen success. Because one person builds one way, does not mean another way is not just as viable as an option. What I am saying is that if you try vendor events, and it doesn't work for you... go back to a script, a kit, and a human. Most builders see success with that model. Again, don't try to learn new skills because the grass appears greener the other way a leader is building. Rely on the gifts the Lord has uniquely gifted you.

What are some of the ways that people are sharing?

♟   Vendor events with flip kits for sale on site (those are starter kits you order in the Virtual Office; then they order on site on a laptop, and ship their kit to you).

♟   Blogging or vlogging the 101 script.

♟   Facebook live classes with the 101 script (in an event or on your personal page).

♟   Instagram or Twitter 101 classes.

♟   Assembling and handing out purple bags with a 101 class cd inside. They "take" the class in their car as they drive away; and you check in.

♟   Textable classes. These are designed for people who are too busy to attend an in-person class. I took the 101 script and the 102 Toxin Free Life script into a professional radio studio and recorded it. (I have been a radio network news anchor for 22 years. That was my pre-Young Living life!). Simply copy the free link, text it to them, have them listen as a podcast on their cell phone as they drive. Then engage in strong follow up. You can find these classes for free at oilabilityteam.com under the "share" button.

♟ DVD classes. I also recorded a DVD of the 101 class for people who are too timid to teach. It has the bold close built in; so you don't have to feel "salesy". Simply play hostess, get a diffuser going, share your story for two minutes, pop the DVD in, and have a laptop where they can sign up at the end of class.

♟ Speed oiling classes. For this, set up stations with the starter kit across the room. Each station takes a couple oils and a paragraph from the 101 class; and the room moves around, set to a timer.

♟ Informal sharing. Simply listen to needs, get oils on people, and loan your stuff out. Wear your oils so they initiate conversations. Carry purple bags so you're prepared.

♟ Make and take classes using only the DIY kit off the Young Living website (and only oils from the starter kit). Teach the 101 and drive to the kit. All your supplies are in one place, in the DIY kit.

♟ NingXia classes, Thieves classes, or Savvy Minerals makeup interactive classes. There are four starter kits in Young Living: The 12 oils in the original kit, the Thieves kit, the Savvy kit and the NingXia kit. Because all four kits lead to wholesale memberships and 24 percent off your oils for life, all four are a viable options for teaching. If a person is not ready to learn oils yet, start with toxic cleaning supplies; and train on the Thieves line. Start with makeup or nutrient rich NingXia as a supplement. You can also start where they are. I would *not* start with Oils of Ancient Scripture or the Feelings kit. There are no starter kits for those bundles; and your oiler is less likely to get a wholesale membership. You want longevity from them. The more discounts they get, the longer they will stick around. Always lead with one of the four starter kits.

There are many more ways of sharing, but those hit some of the main ones. If you don't have luck at several of these, I'd start to ask yourself "why?". Are you giving too many things away, and being shy with your "close"? Are you following up and touching base quickly enough? Are you confident? Are you leading with them, and not with you? Are you listening to their needs? Remember all the things we've trained about in this little book heading into any class you teach. Education over sales. People over profit. Love people more than your fear.

CHAPTER 10

DO NOT GIVE UP!

The whole secret to network marketing really isn't about how fast you share, how many people are in your friend circle, if you live in an urban area, how much knowledge you have, how wealthy you are, how much time you have, if your spouse isn't supportive to start, or if you're overwhelmed. None of that really matters. There are a lot of Royal Crown Diamonds that began overwhelmed. That's why I wrote this little book, with everything in one place, to give you a simple non-overwhelming starting place.

Do you know what the real secret to the whole thing is? Be consistent and don't quit. Be coachable and willing to learn. Consistency pays off a lot more than a couple seasons of hustle. This business is built brick by brick, and conversation by conversation. Silver doesn't happen with five classes or ten "yes's". It happens with the building of a legacy over time. If you can learn the art of getting back on the horse each time you feel you have failed, you have learned a critical piece to make this work. The ones that get to Diamond aren't rock stars. They are the ones that never quit and never stop learning.

Below is a graphic that shows you the tale of two leaders on my team. The first leader taught two classes in a year, then did a couple of one on ones, but at least four months out of twelve she fell off the horse. Person two taught one class a week, without fail, 52 weeks a year. Sometimes there were no-shows; and sometimes there were 12 leaders on a couch. But no matter what, she had one class every seven days on her calendar. The graphs speak to growth without me saying a word. Consistency is the key to your business.

Person 1:

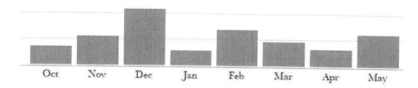

Person 2:

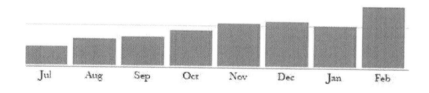

It doesn't matter if you've been Executive for ten years, or if someone put this book in your hands and your starter kit hasn't even shown up yet. The only difference between where you're at right now and the Diamonds that have gone before you are that they have had more conversations, more classes, and more kit sales. Focus on volume, don't give up, and keep sharing. That's how you build a solid business. Diamonds are real people, with real kids, real world problems, real struggles building their organizations, real time management issues, and real exhaustion. Yet they still go home after convention, do their own dishes, and pick laundry up off the floor. The one difference is they know how to fight. If you find that fight inside of you... the fight that cries out that you can't stay where you are anymore... you have started building your fire.

If you have no fire left, it's ok! Start with one conversation. Start with a cell phone contact. Start with listening to the needs around you and offering an oil. Begin from that place. That place is enough to get you facing in the right direction. One kit sale will get your mojo moving. You'll feel like you can rock this business world. Focus on one person at a time if you are overloaded. Many leaders have built incredible organizations with one on ones. If that's the place where you begin, it's not the wrong place. The thing is... you need to start.

If you look at your calendar and there are no classes scheduled next month, it is not a rank up month for you. Your rank is directly linked to the number of people that hear that script and hear your story. Get in front of faces and find freedom.

CHAPTER 11

HOW AM I PAID?

Compensation plans can get pretty hairy. I have no embarrassment telling you that math is not my strength. English has always come easy. Let me keep this on the simplest level possible; and then when you're ready for more, you can snag the full *Gameplan* book and really push forward towards your paycheck!

Are you ready?!!!

Side note first: If this is overwhelming, snag the NingXia packets out of your kit, and down them before reading this. NingXia is a berry juice supplement; and it's amazing! If you want an extra treat, freeze them first; and then suck them down. It's like the best ice cream truck visit of your life; but it's good for you!!!

Now... here we go!!!

There are four parts to your check:

♟ Starter Kit bonuses (25 dollars per kit)

♟ Fast Start (another 25 dollars per kit, plus 25 percent of everything they order for the first three calendar months after the purchase of the starter kit)

♟ Unilevel (You're paid eight percent on your level one's, five percent on your level two's; and four percent on your level three's, four's and five's. This is why it's not wise to build really deep. You're not paid that far down; unless it's in Generations, which you don't get until you hit Silver.)

♟ Rising Star bonuses or Generations pay? (Because this is a beginner book, let's focus on Rising Star bonuses). With this bonus you get paid by share, depending on how many steps you complete in your strategy building. For more info on this, go back and take a peek at Chapter Eight). Rising Star can add up to $120 or more, depending on how many steps you complete.

Let me run you through one break down, so you understand how this process works. We're not going to beat a dead horse; and I'm going to try not to confuse you. We'll just keep it really simple.

You hold a class. Four people come. Two people get starter kits. One of those people also orders another 100 dollars in product (above and beyond their kit). Your paycheck that month would be $50 per kit (for starter kit bonuses and fast start); and another $25 for fast start (due to the added 25% bonus for everything they order), equaling a check of $125 from a single class.

If you taught four classes that month and you had the same results, your first check would be 500 dollars. That's not too shabby considering a class takes less than two hours to teach. That's $500 for eight hours of work in a month. I believe in working smarter, not harder. Young Living fits the bill.

Now, if you get those people to sign up for Essential Rewards; and you teach another class the next month, you'll get paid 25 percent on their order, plus any new starter kit bonuses and fast start bonuses on new kits. This is because fast start goes for three calendar months. After fast start drops off, they slip into the Unilevel system, where you earn eight percent on your level one's each month. If you had 10 people on your first level, and they all ordered 100PV a month; you'd get 80 dollars of residual income for doing nothing. This is simply because they continue to order products for their home long after you taught that first class. You can see how having a team of 10,000 can really pay a hefty check when you calculate all four parts and review them in comparison to your paycheck. If you are teaching one class per week, you are constantly bringing new people into your organization, and constantly growing. One word: if you are teaching for a new leader, and they are ordering 100PV, us their sponsor and enroller number for the kit sale. You know where this goes. You want them to see the check so they teach too. The most powerful tool you have is duplication. Show them the check.

That's how this works. It's AWESOME!!!

CHAPTER 12

THE TWO MOST IMPORTANT BUTTONS IN THE VIRTUAL OFFICE

There are a lot of buttons in the Virtual Office, (your dashboard for all things Young Living). You can run an international multi-million dollar business from that one screen to email leaders, watch rank ups, check Essential Rewards, tabulate your own rank, get training from YL University, and study the products. I'm not going to overload you here. However, I will tell you the two most important buttons:

- How you watch YOU

- How you watch your team

Button #1: let's start with how you watch you.

When you first log in, there is a button right in the middle of the top of the page that says, "Rank Qualification." Click on that. Let me break down how to watch your own personal numbers.

Rank Qualification

I explained earlier that there are nine ranks in Young Living. You can see them across the top of the screen. It begins with Distributor (the starting place) before you earn higher ranks. Then it grows to Star, Senior Star, etc...

There are four things that you must do to hit each rank. Each of these four things are their own row in the graphic above. Row one (left to right) is what you must spend to get fully paid. Row two is your overall OGV. Row three are your legs. And row four is PGV. Let's break it down.

♟ **Row 1:** You must spend 100PV to get your full check. The first row of squares shows 100PV. When you go all the way to Royal Crown Diamond, it's still 100PV. You do not need to spend more when you rank.

♟ **Row 2:** You must hit certain benchmarks for OGV. A Star needs to do 500PV in volume every month to achieve that rank. It resets on the first of each month. A Senior Star needs 2,000OGV in volume each month; an Executive needs 4,000OGV each month. Silvers need 10,000OGV monthly. Golds need 35,000OGV monthly. Platinums need 100,000OGV monthly; Diamonds need 250,000OGV monthly; Crown Diamonds need

750,000OGV monthly; Royal Crown Diamonds need 1.5 million OGV monthly. It sounds like a lot, but I can tell you I would never have hit 10,000 OGV without my team. It's not all about you. It's about the people you know, your warm and cold market, and friends of friends. That's how you blow your business out of the water. If you are consistent, and you are doing activities that actually enlarge your business, you will be surprised at how fast your OGV grows.

♟ **Row 3:** Legs. These are a person and a team, remember? You don't need your first legs until you hit Executive. Then you need two of them. The rest of your volume can be outside the legs; but you must have at least 1,000PV in volume under each leg. Silvers advance those two legs in volume and take them to 4,000OGV. Golds need three legs at 6,000OGV. Platinums need four legs at 8,000OGV. Diamonds need five legs at 15,000OGV. Crown Diamonds need six legs at 20,000OGV. Royal Crown Diamonds need six legs at 35,000OGV. If you are consistently teaching four to six classes a month, OGV can usually grow quickly. Especially if you model the behavior of sharing regularly with your team. Legs are usually the harder of the two to grow, because they require strategy. You must spin one plate, walk away from it, spin another plate, and then return to the original team and work with them if the pace of growth slows down. Ideally, your legs and your OGV cross at about the same time if your team is well strategized. That way, you're not waiting on one or the other. This takes a bit of juggling.

♟ **Row 4:** PGV. This is the fourth line; and it stands for Personal Group Volume. We already covered all the more difficult stuff. This is simply volume in your organization that's outside your qualifying legs. You may need 10,000OGV to be a Silver; but your legs need only be 8,000 of the OGV, which is 4,000 on each leg. The volume outside of those legs would be PGV. Once you hit Silver, you must have at least 1,000PGV outside of your legs.

SIMPLE RULES ON HOW TO RANK:

I have a couple rules I follow to ensure that I'm not waiting on legs or OGV to cross; but my team is well-strategized.

I never build more than two ranks ahead. If I'm a Star, two ranks ahead would be Executive. Focus on the two legs needed for that rank, not legs five and six. Note: I am not speaking against Rising Star. It's different building a leg to 300PV versus taking to 1,000 or 2,000PV.

I don't build too wide or too deep.

I make sure to keep my class count at four to six a month, and train my leaders to do the same.

If a leg has about 10 leaders sharing every month, I feel pretty safe putting my attention on another leg. If I'm not there yet, I'm not there. Keep teaching until the leaders pop up. One of the biggest complaints that I hear is that you don't have enough leaders. The average Silver has a team of 100; and standard network marketing numbers show that 92% of your team are product users. That means a Silver only has eight to ten leaders actively sharing. In most cases, you just haven't taught enough classes yet to find leaders. Don't get discouraged. Fix the problem: TEACH!

There are a couple of other buttons underneath the graph; but to sum it up, it simply tells you how far away from the next rank you are. It also states what you need to do to get there. The Virtual Office will break down your overall OGV for each of your legs; and show you how much volume you need in each place to rank (with Essential Reward orders pending). There's a quick checklist of all four requirements for each rank to make sure you've not missed something. For those of us that don't "math", this is quite a valuable tool. I look at my Virtual Office several times a day.

Button #2: Watch Your Team

You now know how to keep an eye on your own rank, and what to do to hit the next rank. Always set solid goals for yourself. This way you know what you're fighting for each morning you wake up. If your goal is Senior Star this month, and you're 1,0000GV short, you know you need 10 kits (each worth 100PV), or three people at 300PV on Essential Rewards + your order to make that rank. It will take 3-4 classes to equal 10 kits, depending on class size. If you teach one class per week, you should achieve that goal. Go into each month knowing where you're going. Start building relationships and talking to people the month before, so you don't lose the first week of every month scrambling to get a class on the calendar. Also give people enough time to see it and show up.

Now let's talk about your team. The second most valuable button in the Virtual Office is the "My Organization" button on the left side of the page. It looks like this:

I'm just going to give you a few bullet points on this page; then I want you to go play around in your Virtual Office once your team starts to grow, so you get comfortable keeping an eye on this page. This is the most important window for all things for your team.

👤 Members: tells you how many people are on your team

👤 You'll see yourself on the top line, your Member ID to the right, your personal volume (how much you spent), your team OGV, your current PGV (volume outside your legs), if it's an Autoship, whether or not you are on Essential Rewards, and what date your order processes.

♟ Under the Actions section you can: send an email (the envelope symbol); click on the green head to get all the contact info about your leader (address, phone number, personal email outside the Virtual Office); click on the two heads to see where they are in your organization (who is between you and them); and click on the four stacked lines to see what their "Rank Qualification" looks like. It will tell you how their legs break down, and how far they are from ranking, etc...

♟ If there is a little plus sign next to their name, that means you can expand that team. There are people under your level 1 leader.

♟ You'll see the month in the upper right-hand corner. You can change the month to look at stats dating all the way back to the start of your business. You can see your OGV since you started your business! What are your strong months? What months did you lose rank? Track it all right here.

♟ You can run Reports on your team to see who is on Essential Rewards, who your leaders are, who your new members are, and run overall stats about your team. I geek out over this button; and sometimes lose a lot of time messing around with it.

♟ There is even a map function (next to the date) where you can plot out where all the people on your team live. Do you have a lot of members in Texas? In what states do you not have team members yet? Again, it's another geek moment.

We can go over more features of the Virtual Office; but I don't want to overload you. I saved that for the full *Gameplan* book which you can snag anytime you want further training. For now, watch your rank, and watch your team. If you have no team, teach classes and watch your own Rank Advancement. Plot out your goals. The Virtual Office is a great place to pause and do strategy work.

If this chapter (or any chapter) overwhelms you, the neat thing is that you don't need it to launch your business. A lot of this you can learn as you go. I'm one of those people that needs to play a board game to really grasp how it works. My husband can read the instructions to me for an hour, and I'm totally lost. But once my pieces are on the board, I get it. If you're in that group, get your pieces on the board of your business by grabbing the script at the end of this book and getting it in front of faces. Once you start amassing a team, then a lot of this will make far more sense as you see your numbers grow in your Virtual Office. Don't sweat the small stuff. Sharing is the most important thing right now, not understanding every digital feature.

Keep this focus: Script. Kit. People. Repeat.

Chapter 13

A Few Simple Tools to Get You Started

Hey, I've already tossed a lot at you with the Virtual Office, so why not throw a few more digital gadgets your way? They just make everything easier.

Young Living Training and Education is put out by corporate directly. They have really upped their game when it comes to FDA compliant content. That means they are not diagnosing disease; but they are actually giving you real, true uses of oils. It's not watered down. This page has gotten incredible over the past year. It's safe, solid aromatherapy content to share with your team, without having to reinvent the wheel or come up with new topics constantly. Product education is one of the easiest ways to spike your OGV. By sharing these videos to your team page, corporate does the heavy lifting for you. While we're on the topic of corporate, the Young Living blog, (a website), is fantastic too. Check that out here: youngliving.com/blog. There are thousands of articles to share with your team.

I really do believe in the power of **Oily Tools**, which is now run by Young Living corporate. If numbers make your head spin, just look at one number on the front page of this app: your paycheck, (by rank). If you're going to be a Star that month, have no shame. Set that sucker to Royal Crown Diamond and see what your check would be with that OGV at your current rank. It's ok to dream. There is no shame in having vision. Remember... always look where you're going!

Oily Tools is a cell phone app. Snag it in the app store and download it to your phone. Then geek out at all the buttons. I won't go into it in depth here for the sake of time; but I love to see my Essential Rewards percentages (anything over 30% is good. 40% is great. 50% is rock star status). I love to see the number of people at each rank on my team, and to go into the last window on the menu bar and run a money misser report. This is a report that shows me all the people that won't get paid because they never put in a 100PV order. Then I can contact them and make sure they get a check.

Doing that = OGV.

There are **oils reference guide apps** you can download to your phone so you can look up oils while on the fly, (like the EO Bar and the Reference Guide from abundanthealth4u) or discoverlsp.com.

Oil Ability with Sarah (The *Gameplan* page. Ok... that was a shameless plug. I'll take it on the chin for that one! I get on this page on Facebook every Tuesday night at 8:30 eastern for about 20 minutes and answer your live questions, roundtable style. Let's hang out together!)

This list is by no means comprehensive, but it gives you a good start for oily education.

May I give you a few words of caution here? Don't get lost in things that don't grow your business.

You can educate yourself until the cows come home, and still feel like you don't know enough to start sharing. If you wait until you know it all, you miss out on the blessing of a lifetime: freedom. You miss out on getting to ignore your alarm clock every morning. You miss out on retiring your spouse. You miss out going to bed every night being debt free. You miss out on the joy of anonymous silent giving, living on 10 percent, and tithing 90 percent. You miss out on seeing your family and your leaders rank, and experience the same freedom of buying homes, going debt free, and getting precious family time. You get to watch that every single month for the rest of your life, knowing that your simple "yes" to a starter kit made all the difference for your leaders. You miss out on rest and caring for your body in thorough, relaxing ways. You miss out on date nights without dollar limits. You miss out on corporate pampering at convention and on Diamond retreats. You miss out on deep friendships you never would have had as your leaders labor in the trenches beside you, bonding with you and making memories. You miss out on crossing things off a bucket list that you've had in your head your whole life. You miss out on having the peace that your family is cared for, no matter what happens, every night you rest your head on your pillow. They are safe. All that freedom lies after you share and build your legacy. You never get there if you wait to know it all.

Your focus needs to stay on building OGV and legs. Don't get paralysis by analysis. Go ahead and pop in and take a few minutes to learn, especially as a goal after slaying your day. However, don't lose all of your time on Facebook, websites, and apps. There are only three income producing activities that lead to direct OGV growth; nothing else makes the cut. Teach classes, get people on Essential Rewards, and train your leaders. If you get lost in personal education, whether its product education or business training, you're back to treading water again. You're no longer swimming toward shore. I'm all for a little personal development; but don't use it as a crutch to stop teaching classes. When you stop teaching, you stop growing.

CHAPTER 14

DITCH EXCUSES!

Since I am punching you in the face on distraction, why don't we go a level deeper? You're still reading; so you must be able to take it on the chin!

I want you to have this list of excuses so deeply engrained in your head that when you hear these things slip out of your mouth, cross your brain in moments of weakness (and we all have them); you slap them to the other side of the room. Don't even allow this list in your personal vocabulary.

♟   I don't have time.

♟   I don't have money.

♟   I don't have the right personality.

♟   I don't take care of myself; so I'm not the model of a natural lifestyle.

♟   I can't talk to people.

♟   I don't know anyone.

- ♟ I live in the middle of nowhere.

- ♟ I am too tired.

- ♟ My spouse doesn't support my business.

- ♟ I don't make enough to place my order.

- ♟ No one will listen to me.

- ♟ I have no resources.

- ♟ My upline stinks.

- ♟ I don't have reliable internet.

- ♟ I can't find babysitters to watch my kids.

- ♟ I can't get time off from work to teach.

- ♟ Everyone already has oils (only four in 300, remember?)

- ♟ I can't find a place to teach.

- ♟ I'm too scared to talk to people.

- ♟ I have another job and can't add more to my plate.

- ♟ My family is more important than this business. (You will SEE your family if you pursue this business!)

- ♟ Young Living costs too much. (One class a month has the potential to pay for your Essential Rewards order).

- ♟ I read "xyz" on the internet about Young Living; and it must be true.

- ♟ My family thinks I'm a nutcase for believing in oils. If they won't buy; how can I get strangers to respond?

- ♟ I'm not you.

- ♟ I don't have any fight left. I'm exhausted.

- ♟ Once these "certain things" are over in my life, then I can start.

♟   I don't know enough. What if they ask questions???

♟   I don't like selling stuff.

Add your own excuses to that list! Then write the opposite beside it. That's all I want you saying out loud, and in your head.

Here's the deal: do you like where you are? Is how you're spending your current time going to cross things off your bucket list? Is it going to be 20 years until you're debt free? Are you treading water, drowning, or are you changing your life? You CAN break the generational curse over your family! If anyone said building a Young Living business was easy; they are lying to you. It's hard. There is discouragement. You will be let down. You will feel like leaders are wasting their time with some of their activities. People you think will do excellent will disappear; and people you never expect to start, take off. You will have "no show" classes. People you love won't believe in the power of oils. The "no's" will hurt. You'll have seasons where you feel like nothing is moving, and you're treading water. Expect all of those things with this business. But do not dwell on them. Dwelling and expecting are two different things.

Guess what?! Even with that long list of frustrations, Young Living is still easier in the long run than how you are spending your time now; because that hard work leads to freedom. You have done harder things in your life than teaching a two-hour class each week! You have been through so much more! There is no other way out. Your options are to continue doing what you've been doing; or to start digging an escape path.

Is how you spend your 40-hour work week the way you envision it being spent? If you've been doing it that way for 10 years; and there's been no change, will there be change in the next 10 years? Do you feel valued at your job? Do you have purpose? Are you living paycheck to paycheck, one emergency from disaster? Do you have energy? Are you a slave to your own decisions? Do you feel trapped? Are you weary? Are you stressed? There are many types of poverty.

The only person that can dig you out is YOU!

Every Diamond, Crown Diamond, and Royal Crown Diamond battled most of the items on that list at some point while they were building. I've yet to speak to any Diamond that said it was smooth sailing from the moment they got their kit until their 27-thousand-dollar monthly check was coming in the mail. I've never heard that they had infinite time and resources to build when they did. No one along the way, said, *"Yes, classes were always full and resulted in 100 percent kit sales".* They never had a single person who was on another team show up to their classes; and it was a completely stress-free ride to the top.

You must decide how bad you want this. You must decide how much freedom means to you. You must decide if you're willing to stay where you are forever. Once you make that decision, you will be unstoppable. Failure starts in your head. But you can halt it there. It does not need to own you. You don't need a support system to do this. You just need the willpower to move.

I loved anchoring news. I had a passion for my job. I loved the thrill of the news hunt, and the challenge of racing time; and the thrill of opening a mic to five million people every morning. But I was a slave to the clock. I had nothing left to give my kids or my husband when I returned. It all went to radio. That is a very high price to pay to do something that you love. That leads to regret as your kids start to leave the nest.

Now, nothing owns me. I am free. I fill in because I choose to, not because I need to. The shift happened because of the grace of my Lord and Savior first; and then He led me to Young Living.

You have been given a precious gift in this business. It was not a mistake that you were signed up. You have been blessed with Solomon wisdom when it comes to health and wellness. You have been blessed with conviction. Your words have the power to change the course and direction of lives; and the health of thousands of families. How will you use that gift? Will you squander it away on excuses; or will you stand up and fight for those who don't even realize that what they have in their homes is hurting them?

Most of your business is in your mind. It's what you think you're capable of. The glass ceiling above your head in network marketing is set by you. If you always say you'll "try" to get something done; you've made an excuse before you have even started. Make a list, and make it happen! Set a goal and cross it off. Connect with people. You either do this, or you do not do this. But only you can make that decision. There's no magic Vitality Diamond oil in a veggie cap that will get you there. If I had it, I'd give it to you! It takes rolling up your sleeves and sharing oils with purpose, passion, and consistency to make it happen. If you're willing to put the work in, the rewards are limitless. If not, you'll be watching in the bulrushes instead of being a worker in the field. Your team will pass you by; and you'll watch their freedom, but not your own. It's time to take this seriously. It's time to move.

If you want this, ban excuses and fight for it.

A Word for the Builders That Have Plateaued

This book is designed for anyone that needs a leg up. That means that this may be your first exposure to a Young Living business; or you may have been a Star for ten years. Both places are ok! If you're stuck, take a look at why you're stuck. Have you stopped doing the actions that got you your highest rank? You have heard me say it; but I'll repeat it again here: there are only three things that grow your business: teach classes, get people on Essential Rewards, and train your leaders. Usually when I am talking with a builder that has stalled, I'll hear, "No one is coming to my classes anymore", "I have tapped out my warm market", or "everyone is doing oils." Guys, that falls under the excuses category. None of those statements are true! You have to speak the truth over your business if you want it to grow.

Cover yourself in *Believe* oil and restate your sentences. Then get out there and KNOW you can do this! You have the ability to share. The reality is that if you weren't afraid, you'd have 100 percent market share. Anyone outside your front door is a candidate to invite to an oils class. Anyone!! But you have to get fear out of the way of your freedom; and return to the actions that got you the rank in the first place. Without that, you'll watch your team pass you by. There's no reason for it! This business can be built by anyone who wants it, because they don't quit. It's not necessarily about having the first fire you had when you got your kit. It is about relatability and making connections. If you can stay in that place and connect with people, you have mastered the greatest strategy necessary for this: meeting needs. If it's about them and not you, you have changed the game for your business. It is never about sales. It's about people. We all do the same actions to get to Diamond. We have difference paces, different friend circles, and different strategies; but we all do the same 3 things in various ways. Focus on those three things and your feet will get where you want them to go. Cut out all the extras that are keeping you from freedom; and return to the basics. You *still* have it in you to go all the way. Start by consistently sharing all over again. I started by teaching 4 to 6 classes a month under my Crown Diamond leg 8 weeks ago, and took it from 12,000 to 17,000GV. Teaching works. Brace yourself for a rank up.

CHAPTER 15

THE LEGACY OF GARY YOUNG

I've been in Young Living for four years and have a team of about 10-thousand people. Of those 10-thousand, 61 have been to convention since the inception of my business. 61 out of 10-thousand. I have just one small team in a sea of millions of people using Young Living. I shudder to think of those that never met Gary before he passed, and the millions that have yet to join Young Living that will never know the man that started it all.

So many ask me what he was like. In a word? A grandfather. He was loving. He listened deeply. He gave his time. You were the center of the room. Your thoughts had value.

I don't feel like I can put a quick guide together for a Young Living business without telling you why you must fight so hard to get oils in every home in the world. It's all because of this man's mission. Without Gary, there would be no mass-scale essential oils production. I think of all he touched and created, and how differently our lives would be without this man's genius: the cleaning power of Thieves, the discovery of NingXia, his work on the Frankincense road to bring us single-species pure Frankincense. Gary built it all painstakingly, over decades of trial and error in different states and on different continents. He was always ahead. He was thinking of CBD years before it became mainstream, and Mary found pages of his notes on CBD after his death.

When he built this as a network marketing company, he was thinking of you. He was thinking of how to say thank you to you for sharing oils.

Can I tell you how thankful I am that Gary Young loved us enough that he didn't set Young Living up as a retail store front? Do you know what would have happened if he did? I would still have fallen in love with Young Living. I would still have shared my passion for oils with my family and friends. It would still have broken my heart to see them using toxic chemicals in their cabinets. I would still have spoken out. My family and friends would have ordered; because when I recommend a favorite restaurant or a movie, they take me at my word and try it out. I'm not selling anything to them. I'm recommending a lifestyle choice. However, if Gary had set this up as a retail storefront instead, Young Living would have taken 100 percent of the profits for my labor.

Because Gary loved us so much, he was willing to take it on the chin as a "network marketer" when the field was still socially looked down upon as an inferior business. He did this just to make sure that we got the reward for our hard work. Because of Gary, I can enjoy a Diamond income, four years into my business (the average Diamond makes $35,000 a month, according to the 2017 Income Disclosure Guide). Do you know what that means? It means if something were to happen to my husband John and I, my kids would still be cared for forever. They'd each have at least $7,000 a month, every month, for the span of their lives, if I draw up a will and leave my business to them. That's so much better than a 401k or life insurance, which would run out a year or two after I'm gone. That's security that gives me peace. That's the gift Gary gave us when he structured Young Living this way.

Young Living is Gary's gift to you.

Gary passed away in 2018, and I wish more than anything that you could have known him in person. He was a trailblazer and an educator. He was a master aromatherapist who created unbelievable blends. He learned aromatherapy by sleeping on cold distillery floors in France and studying under the best. Read his story in his beautiful wife, Mary's book "D. Gary Young: World Leader of Essential Oils". This is located in your Virtual Office. What he gave to build this company is stunning. Gary was a pioneer who distilled new oils like Dorado Azul and Palo Santo for the very first time. He hunted pure, untainted land for his farms all across the world. He meticulously planted the crops in the ground over and over again until he found the best space and method to grow them. He took over 20 years to amass the largest global library of oil constituents (the levels that each oil must have to be used best by the body). No one else has our library. No one knows what to check their oils against to know if they are high quality. He scouted multiple continents to find out why the oldest people on earth were living so long. That led Gary to the NingXia wolfberry. He traveled the Frankincense road to bring you the best Frankincense on the globe and he did it before any mass scale oils company was in existence. He was so ahead of his time! Gary was the designer of Seed to Seal; and he was the creator of the distilleries that have set the standard for purity in the oils world. Young Living is doing things no one else has done before. They were the first oils company, globally, to offer over 600 oils and oil-infused products. Before Gary, a family would be good at one oil, or a few oils. Gary brought a large-scale selection of oils singles and blends into the modern world. He made them part of the lingo. People pause before they use things they'd used for 20, 30, or 40 years; and they now reach for oils instead. Not just a few hundred families; but millions of families in Europe, Mexico, Canada, the Philippines, China, Malaysia, Australia, Singapore, and the United States. Gary didn't change a few lives. He caused a shift globally in how we view our wellness. He truly is the father of the modern essential oils movement!

Above all of the amazing things Gary accomplished while he was here, he was humble; and he was unabashed about his faith. That speaks more to me than anything else. He was the first to rise in the morning on the farms and the last to go to bed. He would never ask you to do a job he wouldn't do himself. He built a distillery in northern Canada in minus 40-degree weather, just so we wouldn't go another year without Valor oil. He never complained!

Gary was generous. He was the philanthropist that saw children in Ecuador in a small schoolhouse, with no bathroom, and built a $200 million-dollar school for them. He was the one building homes with Young Living brick makers after the earthquake leveled villages in Nepal. He saw a need and he met it. He did not think about it. He didn't say he'd try to help. He did not stop until it was done!

Gary was the one that stopped a Diamond gala for two minutes, even though a room full of entrepreneurs doing a quarter of a million dollars in sales a month were waiting, to speak to my 10-year-old son. To Gary, every person had purpose. Every person had meaning. A 10-year-old child is just as important as a Royal Crown Diamond generating income for the company he built. If you were in front of Gary, there was no one else in the room. This was not because you were smitten with him, but because he was smitten with you. He saw dreams in you that you couldn't even see for yourself.

Gary was the biggest dreamer I know.

It takes dreams like that to build a 2-billion-dollar oils empire from some lavender seeds smuggled from Europe in a pair of cowboy boots. That was the heart of Gary Young.

Now you know him as I have known him. Gary is the culture of Young Living. It's up to us to make sure he's remembered.

Let me end this chapter with a few of my favorite "Gary quotes". It's the only way I can bring him closer to you, so that you can understand the deep respect that I have for him. This is the man that started it all!

With this business, everything you have in your hands began in his.

"I've had so many distributors come and say, 'Oh Gary. I just don't know how to use the oils.' Open the bottle. Start with that. 'But there's so much to know!' I know! I'm still trying to know! If I had waited until I knew it all, you wouldn't be sitting here today. And probably by the time I leave this life, I'll just be figuring out how little I do know."

"I don't make a product for a profit. I make it for a purpose."

"When life knocks you down, roll over and look at the stars."

"Surround yourself with dream builders, not dream stealers."

"If you're not living on the edge, you're taking up too much space."

This is Gary with three of my kids on a trip I won to Venice as an Executive in 2015. They were 12, 14, and 16. He spoke with each of them privately about the importance of getting their starter kit and launching their business right when they turned 16 years old. He sat there and coached my children on a windy boat deck, even though he was weary. He had just boarded the boat late after visiting the Helichrysum farm in Croatia. He took time, invested in my kids, and taught them how to fish. All three of them are now running Young Living businesses. That's what happens when you invest in people.

I have a challenge for you to help you carry the torch: view every person the way Gary did. View them like they are the most important person in the room. If you run every class like that, you'll have the spirit of Gary Young inside of you. You are carrying Gary's mission of bringing oils into every home in the world.

It won't be hard for you to build a team, because the message is always about meeting the need.

#becauseofgary

CHAPTER 16

FIND YOUR "WHY" + THE GAMEPLAN CHALLENGE

It's time to wrap up this little book. You may not feel it, but you have been on a vast journey. You have so much training behind you already! In fact, you have nearly everything you need right now to start. You are so equipped!

I think all of the Diamonds that started at the very beginning... the "trailblazers". Some taught classes by horseback, with cassette tapes, when the word "oil" only had the words "olive" or "motor" in front of it. So many have paved the way for you; and they had no tools. I am grateful for their journey.

"Essential oil" is now part of the vernacular. You can get cheap oil at the grocery store and online. There are already generic knockoffs. It's become part of who we are. Moms douse their kids in it at the playground. Entire websites are designated to the science and study of oils. New companies pop up every day. But Young Living has recorded its place in history. You are part of the movement! You belong to something special.

To share effectively though, you need one last thing: you need a why.

I mentioned it in the first page of this book. You need a reason to get up every morning and fight for this business. It may be because you believe in clean living; and you are willing to fight for the families around you (even people you do not know). Every person has worth. It may be because you need freedom so desperately for your family, and for yourself. You are drowning; but you know there is a way out. You see it now!

It may be because you are lonely; and your sole reason is the people you will meet, and the person you will become in the process. All of those are perfect "why's."

You need that "why", front and center, each day. If you get distracted, you don't remember to fight. Other things take the place of your business. A year of consistency pays off so much more than a few weeks of hustle. With distraction, you find that you don't really remember what you were doing, or why you began in the first place. For you to get to freedom, whatever freedom looks like for you, you cannot forget where you are going, and why you are going there.

Write it down right now. It's likely going to change as you rank up; and that's ok. It's because you grow. Your purpose changes as you do more, and become more, give more, and pour out more. You change as the Lord gives you more freedom; and you learn to be a steward of more resources. Take a moment, write down your reasons below for reading this book, for considering the business, or for picking the business back up again.

MY WHY:

If you need a few ideas, listen to my story at oilabilityteam.com under "Start Here" and "Sarah's Why." It's free. I'm not the smartest, fastest, one of the first Diamonds, or the youngest Diamond. I'm a homeschool momma of five. I am a little person. I have big dreams; and I make a lot of mistakes. In fact, my first book, *Gameplan*, was a pile of all my mistakes in order to save you time, frustration, and burnout. All I know is that I serve a great big God who loves to do big things with little people. If you have days where you feel little as well, then we're on this road together.

You are not alone.

Don't forget the lessons you've learned in this tiny manual. First, speak life over yourself. All those doubts in the first few paragraphs of this book are gone. There is no place for doubt or fear anymore. Even in the span of a small book, you have changed. You will NOT sell to your friends and family. You are an educator. You believe in Young Living and you CAN afford it. You will have extra income in your home. Your plate is not overflowing, you can juggle it all with grace and ease.

You are enough.

HERE'S A QUICK RECAP OF SOME OF THE *GAMEPLAN* TRUTHS IN THIS BOOK

♟ It comes down to loving people and not giving up.

♟ How you share is not as important as *that* you share.

♟ Become good at your personal story.

♟ It's about loving people more than your fears.

♟ When you open your front door, you see... humans. Talk to the humans.

♟ Why do we shy away from closing? Because it's the part of Young Living that feels "salesy" to us. Don't cut your close. You will drive your new oiler to someone else. You will plant a seed, and others will get the harvest.

♟ The "nuts and bolts" of Essential Rewards: you have to use the products to teach the products.

♟ What does Essential Rewards mean for your business? Everything. It is the cornerstone of all you do. There is no rank up without Essential Rewards. Train the lifestyle, not the starter kit.

♟ A careerbuilder.com survey in 2016 found that one in six Americans were actively looking for a job in the next 12 months. There's no reason they can't be on your team.

♟ Always weigh every minute you spend on your business. Is it a distraction, or will it lead to growth? Can it be copied?

♟ Fill a need that changes the entire game.

♟ It's not about your fear or how you are perceived. It's not even if they say yes or no; because that truly doesn't matter. It's how you mentally handle the outcome of the conversation.

♟ Emotionally detach yourself from the sale of the starter kit.

♟ Be consistent and don't quit. Consistency pays off a lot more than a couple seasons of hustle. This business is built brick by brick, and conversation by conversation. A "Diamondship" isn't built in a day.

♟ If you look at your calendar, and there are no classes on it next month, it's not a rank up month for you.

♟ Don't get lost in things that don't grow your business. You can educate yourself until the cows come home, and still feel like you don't know enough to start sharing. If you wait until you know it all, you miss out on the blessing of a lifetime: freedom.

♟ You must decide how bad you want this. You must decide how much freedom means to you. You must decide if you're willing to stay where you are forever. Once you make that decision, you will be unstoppable.

♟ Failure starts in your head. You can stop it there. It does not need to own you.

♟ Young Living is Gary's gift to you.

♟ View every person the way Gary did. View them like they are the most important person in the room. If you run every class like that, you have the spirit of Gary Young inside of you. You are carrying Gary's mission of bringing oils into every home in the world.

♟ The message is always about meeting the need.

♟ Script. Kit. People. Repeat.

OILS FOR BUSINESS

Gary Young oiled up before the start of every day. Be a product of the product, by using the oils you so deeply believe in. The following are my favorite oils for growing a Young Living business: (put them on your feet, big toes, and the back of your neck; or cup your hands and smell them).

<u>In the starter kit:</u> Valor, Frankincense, and Stress Away

<u>For your Essential Rewards order:</u> Northern Lights Black Spruce, Present Time, Highest Potential, Abundance, Believe, Magnify Your Purpose, Geneyus, Oola Grow. I also love NingXia, Nitro, and Mindwise for speaking.

WHAT'S NEXT?

This whole book is for naught if you don't apply one defining principle: connect with people. Take the scripts in the appendix and connect with someone daily; whether it's a text message, a conversation in a hallway at a school, a note on social media, or through a cell phone app. That's how you fill classes. Without connections, they will be no-shows.

Teach with purpose. Do not give handouts of your time and resources. If you get lost for a while, it's ok. Everyone falls off the horse at some point. That does not mark you for failure. The only ones who fail at this business are the ones who give up. Don't let one month of empty classes lead to five months of empty classes. Don't let five "no's" shut your business down. Don't let 100 "no's" shut your business down. Just evaluate how you're connecting with people. How are you perceived? Are you meeting their needs? Did you touch base? Did your message come through? Did you meet them where they are? Did you listen? Were you timid in your close? Did you plant seeds that someone else got to harvest? Give yourself an honest self-evaluation.

You were made for more than "no". The biggest determination of the length of time it will take you to get to Diamond is how quickly you get back on the horse and never, give up!

May I issue one last challenge?

There's no more homework and no more practice. You have all the training you need for right now. You know enough to launch. You know enough to slay your business. If you stay laser-focused on teaching classes, educating people in the lifestyle of Essential Rewards, and training your leaders, your business will look radically different one year from now.

What's the challenge? Well, I have a name for it.

The Gameplan Challenge

I call it the *Gameplan* challenge, and I give it to all my boot-campers who are finishing the full *Gameplan* book and workbook. Here you go:

- *Make it a goal to **teach a class a week** for the next 52 weeks.*

- *For every person that gets a kit, sit down with them and **train Essential Rewards**.*

- *Every time someone expresses an interest in the business, **give them this book**.*

- *Commit to those 3 actions for the next 12 months, consistently.*

Give this business one year of your life and see where it goes. On my own team, those that take the *Gameplan* challenge usually jump at least one rank, and sometimes two or three ranks, in the span of that year. Their lives are changed forever. It's not because of a book, but because of their own action. Are you doing the things that grow your business, or are you wasting time? You can ignite your business TONIGHT. You can send your first text and make your first connection. You can invite your best friend or mom to your living room couch. Your first class could be before you lay down to rest this evening. You determine the pace of your growth. You dictate how your business will go down.

Just start.

There is no place for fear!

I promised that you could ignite your business in two hours. I meant it. You have more knowledge in this tiny little guide than most of the Diamonds had when they started. All you need, now, is to put it into practice. If you wait until you have more aromatherapy or business training, or until people start coming to you; you're delaying your rank up. Peek at that list of excuses one more time. Then ban it forever. Never let any of those words leave your lips.

You are *unstoppable!*

Can you share oils today? Can you share again this week? Can you share with consistency? Can you love people even when you are afraid? That simple step of sharing, over and over again, is what will get you the rank. It's not all the bells and fluff. It's just you, your kit, a script, a person, passion, and compassion. Begin immediately. Start while the fire in you is burning, and the goals are hot and your focus is unwavering. Start when your "why" is pounding in your head, and you need freedom *now,* and distractions and fear haven't gripped you. Start and never stop until you hit Royal Crown Diamond.

I have three final thoughts for you.

♟ *Don't overthink this.* Grab the script and teach a class. If that's your starting place and you're there for months, it's good enough. Don't worry about IPA's, checklists, and training leaders if you're on overload. Just share.

♟ You have more in you than you think you do. Just set aside an hour or two a week, and share. The number of classes you hold is directly linked to the amount of time you will spend in the land of crazy. If you want the stress in your life to die down, you must start building. You don't need to commit 40 hours a week to your Young Living business; but you do need to share with people as often as you can. If that takes on the form of textable classes this month with a few responses in your spare moments, it's still connecting. Give what you can, but be consistent.

One more thing...

♟ You are **worthy.**

You are worthy of the crown. Be confident when you share. This business is about LOVE. It's about education. People are searching for what you have to offer. Your knowledge is valuable.

Now go tell the world. Freedom is not as far away as it may feel!

Begin TONIGHT.

It's time to share.

It's time to grow.

It's time to carry oils to every home in the world...

Because of Gary.

APPENDICES

WHY SCRIPTS?

Why do I use scripts? Because nearly every major successful network marketer does: Eric Worre, Dani Johnson, etc... Scripts can be copied; and that makes it easier for your leaders to lead. I am not a master at network marketing. I am a mom. To understand how this works, I had to study the success of those who have gone before me. Japan recovered after World War II by emulating the strengths of a dozen countries around the world. I studied 42 of the best network marketing books, and all of them used scripts. A script is simple and it works. You have two scripts in this book, the 101 and the 102: Toxin Free Life, and finally, the Bold Close, which can be tacked onto the back of any script. It does not mean you skip your story. That's the most important part! Facts tell and stories sell. Start with your story and then read the script. If you train using scripts, anyone on your team will have the words to share.

SIMPLE 101 SCRIPT
BY YOUNG LIVING DIAMOND SARAH HARNISCH
TAKEN FROM THE 2ND EDITION OF GAMEPLAN

Note: Start with your story! What got you into oils? What were your "wow" moments? Share that first. Then come up with your own personal stories for several of the oils at the end of the script.

WHAT ARE ESSENTIAL OILS?

They are the most powerful part of the plant.

They are distilled from shrubs, flowers, trees, roots, bushes, fruit, rinds, resins, and herbs.

Oils consist of hundreds of different natural, organic compounds.

In humans, many oils provide support for every system in the body: your skeletal system, muscular system, circulatory system, endocrine system, hormones, respiratory system, and immune system. They support brain health and a healthy weight. They are used extensively for spiritual support in your prayer life, as well as emotional support. They have been used for thousands of years as beauty aids. An oil in a diffuser can soothe a child's tough day at school; and provide a calming effect when you've had a stressful day at work. Oils can be used as an alternative to cleaning chemicals in the home. You can literally start swapping out every single chemical in your home to live a purer lifestyle; and you can do it without breaking the bank!

You do not need to be an aromatherapist to use them. In most cases, just rub it topically into the skin. There are three main ways to get oils into your system: the English apply it topically (rub it on the skin), the French ingest and cook with it; and the Germans diffuse and inhale, which is the most effective method because it doesn't have to pass through the digestive system.

How do they enter? How long do they last?

Tests have shown that oils reach the heart, liver, and thyroid within three seconds when inhaled. They were found in the bloodstream within 26 seconds when applied topically. Expulsion of essential oils takes three to six hours in a normal, healthy body.

ESSENTIAL OILS HISTORY

They were first mentioned by name in the biblical book of Genesis, Chapter 37, when Joseph was sold to the slave traders. They carried spicery, balm, and Myrrh! Genesis ends with the burial of Joseph's father, anointed with Myrrh. There are over 1,100 direct and indirect mentions of essential oils in Scripture.

Some of the oldest cultures on earth used essential oils. The Babylonians used Cedarwood, Myrrh, and Cyprus. The Egyptians used essential oils for beauty and embalming; and they have the oldest recorded deodorant recipe made with essential oils. Pakistan and Rome used essential oils in communal bath houses.

They were even used by Christ! Jesus was given gold, Frankincense, and Myrrh. Frankincense is sometimes referred to as "the coconut oil of essential oils," because it has over 10,000 uses.

Essential oils were used by the Medieval Europeans, many of whom brought oils back during the Crusades.

It was only after World War II when essential oils were "rediscovered." The science on their uses grows with every single year.

DO ESSENTIAL OILS WORK?

I used essential oils before Young Living. Lavender smelled nice in my bath, but never had any significant effect on my body. I bought my lavender online, at farmers markets, or at bulk foods stores. In the United States, there is no rating system for essential oils. It would be wonderful if there were; because then you'd know what you were buying! If you walk into a grocery store and look at a box of cereal, you'll see nutrition facts on the side. There are no "nutrition facts" on the side of oils. That means you must trust the source. You have to know the company you are purchasing from. What sets Young Living aside? Seed to Seal. It's our promise of purity. You can learn more about Seed to Seal at seedtoseal.com. All of our oil is shipped from around the world to Spanish Fork, Utah, where it's run though vigorous 8-point testing to ensure purity. Those tests are run in triplicate at the farm, at Spanish Fork, and a third time before bottling. It's why Young Living has never had a recalled essential oil in over two decades of business. You can trust the integrity. Seed to Seal is based on three pillars: sourcing, science, and standards. Young Living's oils are tested by scientists with over 180 years of combined lab experience. They also do third party testing with two accredited, respected, independent labs.

Young Living is a global leader in essential oils, with nearly two billion dollars in sales annually. Those that use the oils keep coming back! There are three-thousand global employees, 600 life-changing products, 16 corporate and partner farms, more than 20 international markets, 50 highly trained scientists, 12 independent partner labs, and four million global members. What does that mean? The testing is thorough and precise. It's why I don't buy from a mom and pop oils shop. They don't have the team to do the testing that's needed to stay on top of hundreds of oils and blends. They don't have Seed to Seal. You can visit our farms.

Why can't you just buy oils at the grocery store? Purity. You get what you pay for. I have seen bottles of Frankincense for seven dollars at the grocery store; but it costs more than that just to distill! It's a red flag that the oil has been altered in some form.

All oils in the world fall into one of four categories: Authentic, Manipulated, Perfume, or Synthetic.

Authentic means the oils are 100 percent pure, with no added synthetics or other additives in the bottle. These are Young Living oils!

Manipulated means the final product has been made to smell more pleasing and less earthy. Some of the heavier molecules have been stripped out; or another additive introduced, to enhance the aroma.

Perfume oils are not pure. They are mixed with synthetics to enhance the aroma. These oils have no therapeutic action. Frequently, solvents are used to extract the plant.

Synthetic oils are not true oils at all. They smell nothing like the original plant and are typically labeled as "scented products." These are synthetic.

Authentic is the only true pure oil. Synthetic oils would be like opening your fridge, taking a glass of orange juice, and diluting it 95% with chemicals before you drank it! It wouldn't have the same benefits of a full glass of pure orange juice. That's why you want authentic oils. Before you purchase, check to see if the company grows their own plants, has Seed to Seal, and controls the entire process from the farm to the sealed bottle. Pesticides, pollution, previously farmed land... all of it can affect the quality of an oil. Why would you go the extra step of using an oil to get away from a chemical only to use an oil laden with chemicals. It makes no sense.

Young Living's Seed to Seal process is a promise of integrity. There are no pesticides used, no artificial fertilizers, and no weed killers. The plants are harvested at their peak. They're then put through a vigorous testing process. Then they go from the farm directly to your home. Seed to Seal is not a slogan, it's a promise.

WHY DO SOME OILS COMPANIES SELL OILS CHEAPER THAN OTHERS?

Most essential oils are sold cheaper than others because companies cut corners to save money. If you spray your crop with pesticides, you have more crop to distill. If you use a chemical solvent to extract the oil, you pull more out. If you dilute it with a cheaper oil, or a carrier oil, you stretch the oil you have distilled, and can easily sell it cheaper.

HOW OILS ARE MADE:

It takes a great deal of work to produce a tiny amount of essential oil!

60,000 rose blossoms provide only one ounce of Rose oil.

Lavender is abundant (220 pounds will provide seven pounds of oil).

Jasmine flowers must be picked by hand before the sun becomes hot on the very first day they open, making it one of the most expensive oils in the world! It takes eight million hand-picked blossoms to produce 2.2 pounds of oil.

A Sandalwood tree must be 30 years old and 30 feet high before it can be cut down for distillation. Gary Young's Sandalwood trees must be 90 percent dead before they are harvested.

A little goes a long way. Most oils are $10 to $30 a bottle. Depending on oil thickness (viscosity), a 5-ml bottle contains about 90-100 drops; and a 15-mL bottle contains about 200-240 drops. Each application is one to three drops, meaning even a small bottle will get you 45 to 90 applications. Thieves cleaner is made of plants only; and it costs about $1.50 a bottle to make. You can't even get that in the organic section at the grocery store! It replaces a multi-purpose cleaner, glass cleaner, and floor cleaner. The organic versions of those can run you four to six dollars a bottle. Thieves cleaner and Thieves hand sanitizer come in the starter kit. That's where I began my oils journey, and where I recommend you start yours.

ARE THEY SAFE?

There are certain oils that are photosensitive, meaning you don't want to wear them and go outside. These are mostly citrus oils, like Citrus Fresh, Lemon, etc.

When using on your skin, always watch for redness and dilute with a carrier oil. Dilute oils on children, because their skin is more permeable and absorbs the oils more quickly. What is a carrier oil? It's a fatty oil like olive oil or coconut oil, and its molecules are much larger than those of essential oils. Using a carrier oil with an essential oil slows down the rate the body can absorb the essential oil, because it must ping pong through the large molecules of the carrier oil to get into your skin

Be wary of putting the oils topically near your eyes. Some oils, like Peppermint, can cause a burning sensation. If you are placing an oil near your eye, apply the oil to a Q-tip instead of tipping the bottle toward your face.

You can become desensitized to an oil if you use the same one day after day. I rotate my oils every three to four days.

What about internal use of essential oils? NAHA, one of the top aromatherapy organizations in the United States, doesn't advocate essential oils for internal use. Why? Most oils companies don't carry any GRAS (Generally Regarded as Safe) essential oils. Many argue that internal essential oil use is unsafe; and I would agree, in some circumstances. You need to make sure you're checking the labels first. Young Living Vitality oils are approved for internal use, just like a food additive. You have been consuming essential oils internally for most of your life, for instance: when you chew gum, or put Oregano in your pasta.

NAHA also bases a lot of their decisions on the British model, which advocates topical use only. Many of the British studies are flawed. For example: done at extremely high doses, or in ways the oils aren't used. Young Living utilizes all three methods, British, French, and German. The French have been safely using some essential oils internally for decades. Young Living's Vitality line has distinctive white labels so you can easily recognize which oils are safe to take internally.

ON THE FLIP SIDE...

Look at the ingredient list of what you have in your bathroom and kitchen. Every day we put products on our skin, in our body, and breathe them in; but many of these products contain damaging chemicals. The average woman applies over 300 chemicals every day to her body just through soaps, makeup, shampoos, and hair care products. Eighty of those products are applied before breakfast!

When you use Young Living's essential oils, you're using a product with one ingredient, like: Lemon, Oregano, or Tangerine. No synthetic additives and no yuck.

Is all this a bit overwhelming? Let me tell you how I started my oils journey: with a Young Living Starter Kit. It's the only item on the Young Living website that is half off! If you're a frugal momma like me, this is the best bang for your buck! Let's run through the oils in the kit.

(Pass around the Premium Starter Kit with Diffuser, open the bottles, and smell them.)

Frankincense. One of the top skin oils. It helps smooth the appearance of skin. A key ingredient in Young Living's "Brain

Power" essential oil blend. Diffuse during prayer time to help with grounding and purpose.

Lavender. Oil of relaxation. Diffuse for a calming, soothing aroma. Unwind by adding a few drops to a nighttime bath. This is one of the top oils to support healthy skin. It's referred to as the "Swiss army knife" of essential oils because of its many uses. I love this for bruises, blisters, rashes, bug bites, and burns.

Peppermint Vitality. It helps support gastrointestinal comfort. It pro- motes healthy bowel function and enhanced healthy gut function. It helps maintain efficiency of the digestive tract. It may support performance during exercise. I call this my "highway hypnosis" oil because 1 drop keeps me alert while driving.

Citrus Fresh Vitality. Diffuse to freshen the air. This blend is a mix of Orange, Tangerine, Grapefruit, Lemon and Mandarin oils. It's a replacement for chemical-based home fragrances. Spritz in rooms and closets and over linens. Dilute with V-6 carrier oil, and use a perfume. It also helps to tone and smooth the appearance of skin. This is a powerful oil for immune support.

Thieves Vitality. Helps support a healthy respiratory system; and it helps maintain overall wellness when taken as a dietary supplement. Add a drop to hot drinks for a spicy zing! This is the first oil I use when I feel like I am "coming down" with something. Gargle with it in water.

Peace and Calming. This is one of my favorite kid oils! Though I have been known to sneak a few drops onto my hands and enjoy it as well! I use it to bring peace to the chaos in my head. It's different than Stress Away in that Stress Away is for prolonged use during the day, and specifically for the sort of "fight or flight" stress that comes on fast. Peace and Calming is more for the evening to slow your mind down. Peace and Calming contains Ylang Ylang, Orange, Tangerine, Patchouli, and Blue Tansy.

Stress Away. This promotes wellness and may be an important part of a daily health regimen. It's one of the top emotion oils blends! I use Stress Away before the onslaught of a heavier day. This oil contains Lime, Copaiba, Vanilla, and is like a massage for the senses.

Lemon Vitality. Its citrus flavor enhances the taste of food and water. The key ingredients are Thieves and NingXia Red. It may help support the immune system. Use it to get sticky goo off your hands or skin or to degrease pans.

PanAway. Apply after exercise to soothe muscles. It has a stimulating aroma. Apply to the back and neck for a soothing aromatic experience. It supports the appearance of healthy skin coloration. Also great for headaches.

DiGize Vitality. This is the top oil blend for supporting the digestive system. Add two drops, along with a drop of peppermint, to water for a stimulating beverage. Take in a veggie capsule internally. Use with Essentialzyme at every meal to support a wellness regimen.

Raven. This is a cleansing blend of Ravinsara, Peppermint, Eucalyptus Radiata, and other essential oils. Raven creates a cooling sensation when applied topically to the chest and throat. Diffuse up to three times daily for a soothing aroma. This oil changes the game for anything involving breathing.

Valor. Valor contains Black Spruce, Blue Tansy, Camphor Wood, Geranium, and Frankincense. The Valor blend was used by the Ancient Romans in the bathhouses before they sent their soldiers into battle. Its smooth, relaxing scent is designed for courage and bravery.

The kit now comes with 12 bottles of oil, a diffuser, 2 packets of NingXia, a packet of Thieves cleaner, 2 aromaglide roll-on caps that turn your bottles into instant roll-ons, and a Thieves hand sanitizer, for $165.

How do you order? Simply go to www.youngliving.com, click on "Become a Member," and use the number of the person who told you about oils as enroller and sponsor. It's that simple. Welcome to the world of oils!

Note: end with the Strong Close script from *Gameplan!*

Get this as a textable class for free at:

oilabilityteam.com/share under "classes"

SIMPLE 102 SCRIPT:

TOXIN FREE LIFE (THIEVES)
BY YOUNG LIVING DIAMOND SARAH HARNISCH

Why Natural Health Is So Important

The number two cause of death in the United States is cancer. Cancer expenditures in 2011 were 88 billion dollars. 1,620 people a day die of cancer. One in three men will have cancer by age 60 in the United States, and one in five women. There are 10-thousand new cases a year among children. One in three cases in the U.S. are directly linked to poor diet, physical inactivity, weight, or chemical exposure. The American Cancer Society says that only five to ten percent of all cancer cases are from gene defects. Five percent! That means 95 percent of cancer cases are under our control. It's what we allow into our homes.

The National Institute of Occupational Safety and Health studied 2,983 ingredients in our products at home and found 884 toxic ingredients. The shocking studies showed that: 314 of them caused biological mutations; 218 caused reproductive problems; 376 caused eye and skin irritation; 778 were toxic to the human body; 146 (they knew) caused cancerous tumors; but they were allowed in the United States, even though they were banned in other countries around the world. These chemicals are allowed in nearly every type of cleaning supplies in the United States (common things under your cabinets right now). Even organic cleaners have some known carcinogens that are just naturally derived.

Twenty-six seconds after exposure, chemicals are found in measurable amounts in the human body. The average woman applies 300 chemicals to her body a day (80 before breakfast). The top 10 most dangerous chemicals in our home: air fresheners, like plug ins or candles. Chemical cleaning supplies for your counters, floors, toilets, drain and oven cleaners, furniture polish, dishwasher soap, and dish soap are also culprits. It also includes beauty supplies and personal care products such as: hairspray, gel, shampoo, and deodorant. Deodorant with aluminum is one of the leading causes of Alzheimer's and Parkinson's disease in the United States. One of the top pollutants in the family home is laundry soap and fabric softener which you wash your clothes with, and put on your skin. It outgases in your closet all night long. That information, is based on a study from the U.S. Environmental Protection Agency's Top 10 Killer Household Chemicals.

What happens when your body is chemically overloaded? You may see it as something as catastrophic as cancer. Most of us feel it in other ways: lethargy, inability to focus, sleep trouble, chronic inflammation, unexplained pain, fibromyalgia, skin issues, adult acne, hormones, hot flashes, stress, anxiety, and fear. If you face any of these issues, it's time to kick chemicals to the curb. You can control what you allow within the walls of your home.

The average Diamond makes $35-thousand-dollars a month, according to the 2017 Young Living Income Disclosure Guide. This is just by teaching people to live a chemical free lifestyle. There is a little a book about one Young Living Diamond named Sarah Harnisch that can show you how simple it is to get your oils for free. It's called Gameplan: Build A Life Beyond Survival Mode. I have a copy of that book for you to take home for free today.

Young Living is an essential oils company based out of Utah. It remains the largest essential oils company in the world, and a pioneer in the art of organic distillation. Their methods have been copied all over the globe. They produce the most oils on the planet; and they do it right through their Seed to Seal process. If you want to learn more, I have recorded several lectures to DVD or audio cd. I'd recommend the 101 lecture, a ground up, fast-paced study on all things oils for the new oiler.

Why am I so passionate about getting rid of chemicals? Let me share my story.

(Share your story)

What are essential oils?

They are the most powerful part of the plant (the lifeblood of the plant). They repair and restore the plant when it is attacked or injured. In the human body, they have access to the limbic lobe of the brain. That part of the brain controls heart rate, breathing, memory, hormones, stress levels, and blood pressure. Oils are tiny (smaller than viruses). They hit your cells in 3 seconds when inhaled, and 26 seconds when applied topically. In the first week that I had my kit, I used it over 80 times successfully.

Why would you want oils in your home? Oils have no yuck. They are just the distilled plant in steam form. There are millions of uses such as: to support systems in the human body like your cardiovascular system or your endocrine system, (which effects hormones) supporting your joints, your brain, or liver. They are used to replace chemical cleaning supplies. Thieves cleaner is all I use to wipe down my bathrooms, my stove, and my kitchen. I mop my floors with it even. It's made of plants and five essential oils. You can use oils to replace your personal care products. Young Living has an entire line of shampoos, soaps, conditioners, eye creams, and face washes that are completely chemical free. If you use oil infused supplements, you get the benefit of the supplement along with the power of the oil. Young Living has the best protein powder I've ever seen. Protein is brain food that helps you think clearly and lose weight.

It matters where the oils are sourced. There are four types of oils on the earth:

- ♟ Grade A: **Authentic**
- ♟ Grade B: **Manipulated**
- ♟ Grade C: **Perfume**
- ♟ Grade D: **Synthetic**

It's so important that you only use grade A oil because of the concentration in the bottle. It's like eating an entire apple tree sprayed with pesticide, instead of one apple. It makes no sense to go the extra mile to get away from chemicals, and then use an oil laden with chemicals.

There are 100-thousand chemicals on the market today. The Toxic Substance Control Act of 1976 grandfathered them in. What does that mean to you? Simply put: these chemicals have not had any safety testing, and we know very little information about their side effects. Of the chemicals tested, toxic labeling is only required if 50 percent or more of the animals tested die. Under the TSCA, manufacturers are protected by secret trade laws that allow them to keep their ingredients lists a secret. Dr. Samuel Epstein, chairman of the Cancer Prevention Coalition, says, "It is unthinkable that women would knowingly inflict such exposures on their infants and children and themselves if products were routinely labeled with explicit warnings of cancer risks. But they are not labeled."

Since the 1940's, prostate cancer is up 200 percent; thyroid cancer is up 155 percent; brain cancer is up 70 percent; breast cancer i sup 60 percent; and childhood cancer is up 35 percent. The American Cancer Society estimates a 50 percent rise in cancer rates by 2020. The quality of air inside your home is five to seven times more toxic than outdoor air quality. Chemical household cleaning product sales were a seven-billion-dollar industry in 2007.

This is something you NEED to take seriously! No one is watching your home but you. You are the gatekeeper. I'd be willing to bet my life that there are things in your home right now that you're exposed to every single day that could be killing you. The thing is, it's preventable.

Where do you start?

Start small. Start slow. Start with what you're convicted on. Let me give you a simple tip. With your food, simply start by reading the ingredients. If you can't pronounce it, don't eat it. It doesn't mean you can't have ice cream; just go for the ice cream with milk, sugar, eggs, and vanilla, instead of an ingredients list of 35 items you can't even pronounce.

With your home, start with the biggest offenders first. Start with laundry soap, dishwasher soap, cleaning supplies, candles, and plug ins. Toss candles and plug ins. Swap them out with a diffuser and a pure essential oil. Young Living has oil infused Thieves cleaner, laundry soap, and dish soap that are affordable and simple to use.

If you're a bit overwhelmed, grab my 101 lecture on DVD. Learning to integrate oils into your home is about small, simple, baby steps. Take it one month at a time. Maybe the first month you focus solely on Thieves cleaner; and toss every chemical cleaning supply under your sink. Go home and wipe your kitchen down and fall in love, knowing you just boosted your immune system instead of taxing your liver. Thieves cleaner costs one dollar a bottle to make at home. One $22 bottle of cleaner gets you 30 spray bottles. Add one capful to a spray bottle of water and you're off and running. It's the cheapest organic cleaner out there.

The next month, swap out some laundry soap or dish soap. Month three, focus on your personal care products, like deodorant, and shampoo. Month four, focus on beauty supplies, like face wash. Every day you leave your makeup on, your skin ages by seven days. Use a chemical free option to get it off.

I started this journey, myself, with a Young Living starter kit and have never looked back. We use the oils every single day in our home. Every oil you use is a chemical you're not using. This is where I began; and it's where I'd recommend you start.

Young Living has made an entire Thieves premium starter kit specifically centered around cleaning supplies. It's a simple, easy way to work your way into oiling.

The Thieves starter kit comes with:

- 15-ml Thieves
- Thieves AromaBright™ Toothpaste
- Thieves Fresh Essence Plus Mouthwash
- 2 Thieves Cleaner
- 2 Thieves Foaming Hand Soap
- 2 Thieves Spray
- 2 Thieves Waterless Hand Purifier
- 5-ml Stress Away™
- AromaGlide™ Roller Fitment that turns any bottle of oil into a roll-on
- 10 Sample Packets of essential oils: Thieves, Lemon, Peppermint, Lavender, and Peace and Calming.

That means you get Thieves essential oil, toothpaste, mouthwash, cleaner (which replaces all the cleaner in my home) hand soap, spray that you can use for shopping carts or airplane seats (or to spray your kids hands down in a restaurant before you eat), and hand purifier.

What is Thieves cleaner used for? Here are 12 ideas:

- Put it undiluted into a roll-on and make a stain stick for your clothing with no chemicals.

- Pour it onto spots on your carpeting undiluted and get rid of stains.

- Let it sit on pots and pans with burnt food stuck to the bottom of them.

- Put a cap of it in a spray bottle of water and use it as surface cleaner for your kitchen, bathroom counters, sinks, your stove, or your bathtub.

- Add some to a bucket of hot water and mop your floors with it.

- Put a little Thieves cleaner in some baking soda and make your own soft scrub without any chemicals that you can use in your oven.

- Refresh a musty carpet by putting Thieves oil in some baking soda, let it absorb, and then sprinkle it over your carpets.

- After washing your clothes with Thieves laundry soap, add four to five drops to a dry washcloth and toss it in the dryer to make your clothes smell fresh.

- Put one drop of Thieves on anything sticky stuck to an object or kid, and wipe it off. It gets rid of residue.

- Clean your dishwasher by running an empty cycle with vinegar and two drops of Thieves oil.

- Add a drop to the cardboard insert of your toilet paper rolls to have Thieves freshness in your bathroom.

It's some of the best glass cleaner replacement I've ever seen. Spray it right on your windows to take gunk off. It's also great for detailing cars and cleaning the dashboard.

There is no yuck in Thieves; just plants and plant-based materials. You can literally replace everything under your counter with one bottle.

What about Thieves oil? Why would you want that? The oil is a lot more concentrated than the Thieves cleaner. Thieves oil doesn't contain the other plant ingredients that allow the oil to be evenly spread through the cleaning solution; so if you make it at home with straight up oil you'll end up with oil and water.

Five Uses for Thieves essential oil:

- Put some on your feet and spine for immune support. Dilute it with coconut oil if you're putting it on kids.

- Take Thieves vitality internally for the same reason. One of my favorite recipes is 10 drops of Thieves vitality, 8 drops of oregano vitality, and 2 drops of frankincense vitality in a veggie capsule.

- Add a drop of Thieves vitality to the toothpaste on your toothbrush to feel fresh.

- Put it in the diffuser as a favorite fall blend—it has cinnamon and clove in it.

- Clove has a numbing effect to it. I like to put Thieves on my teeth to sooth them when they hurt.

Let's talk for a moment about Thieves and what's in it

The Thieves blend contains clove, eucalyptus, rosemary, lemon, and cinnamon. It's based on the legend of the four thieves in Marseilles, France dating from the time of the outbreak of the bubonic plague. Century after century, from the 1300's to the 1700's, outbreaks claimed up to half the population of Europe. There was a nasty outbreak between 1593 and 1608.

About that time, an aromatic legend developed around a brew called "Marseilles Vinegar" or "Four Thieves Vinegar." The group allegedly confessed they used it with complete protection against the plague while they robbed the bodies of the dead. There are a variety of recipes are out there; but they included dried rosemary tops, dried sage flowers, fresh rue, camphor, garlic cloves and vinegar, which were too steep for seven or eight days to fight, as history has it, the plague. The vinegar was noted in a number of famous medical books published later on, including the Pharmacologia from 1825.

D. Gary Young, founder of Young Living, is the most responsible for the story reaching the legendary status it has today. He created the Thieves blend in 1994 for immune support, as the result of his study at Warwick University in London. Gary said quote, "I must tell you I have read 17 different versions of the Thieves story. Some claim there were four thieves and some claim there were as many as 40. Most of the legends took place in the 15th century, but others put the date in the 18th century. The formulas varied from one story to the next, but through my research, I was led to four key botanicals that were mentioned again and again—clove, cinnamon, rosemary and lemon—four of the same ingredients that make up the Thieves oil blend today."

Young Living doesn't just have the Thieves starter kit; it has an entire line of Thieves products: bar soap, cough drops, dental floss, dish soap and dishwasher powder, mints, veggie soak, and even Thieves wipes. This is a better choice for your family. It's simple, requires no prep, and easy to swap. If affordability is an issue, consider this: When you get a Thieves starter kit, you get 24 percent off your oils for LIFE. It's a wholesale membership. If you sign up for Essential Rewards, (which ships Young Living products you pick out each month on a date you choose) you get 10 percent off right off the bat. That means they are paying you 10 percent back for buying your laundry soap and your dish soap; and there's no chemical yuck inside. After four months, you get 20 percent back. After 25 months, you get 25 percent back, just for buying your cleaning supplies on Essential Rewards. No grocery store that I know of does that!

I've placed a link for you to sign up for a $165-dollar premium starter kit—with over 23 Thieves products and oils inside. Click on it and get started on your Young Living journey. It is one of the best decisions I ever made to live a chemical free lifestyle.

Let's end with why you want oils in your home.

We'll finish with a story of a family with quadruplets. In celebration of the 25-year creation of Thieves, Young Living has put together a two-minute video.

https://www.youtube.com/watch?v=6rwoCPYJCNw

You matter. Your family matters. Your friends matter. You can take control of your own health. You don't have to feel the way you do. You don't have to feel tired, groggy, swollen, exhausted, or sore. Kick the chemicals out of your life and start living clean.

The Bold Close

Let me get real with you for a moment as I wrap up; and tell you the true reason I teach so emphatically about this. Why does chemical-free living matter so much to me? Because I have seen the other end of a chemical filled lifestyle, and I want everyone to know what they are putting in and on their bodies.

The number two cause of death in the United States is cancer. One in three men will have cancer after age 60, and one in five women. The American Cancer Society says only five to ten percent of all cancer cases are from gene defects. Five percent! That means 95% of cancer cases are under our control. It's what we allow into our homes.

You can control what you allow within the walls of your home.

I was invited to my first oils class, got my Starter Kit, and began right where you are now, taking this chemical-free living thing one day at a time; kicking one chemical out of my home at a time. You can do this. It's about taking small steps and saying, *"I will not allow these things in my home"*. You can't control all the places you are exposed—but you are the gatekeeper of your house.

Learn alongside our team. Let us guide you through the process with simple, easy steps. Step one is to start with the starter kit, which includes a diffuser and 12 bottles of oil (some of the most common oils on the earth for supporting systems of the body). They each have just one ingredient! Lemon is just cold pressed lemon rinds. Frankincense is resin, properly steam distilled at the right temperature to make essential oil. Lavender is freshly distilled at the peak of the harvest (with thousands of uses in the home). Let us come alongside you and train you how to kick chemicals to the curb. You CAN do this.

Start by heading to www.youngliving.com, click on "become a member", and enter the sponsor and enroller number of the person who gave you this audio CD. Welcome. I'm glad you're investing in your family!

Once you have put in the sponsor and enroller number, it will take you to a second page and ask for personal information where you'll set up your account. Write it all down so you're able to log in later. The third page asks which Starter Kit you want. My personal favorite is the desert mist diffuser with the Premium Starter Kit. If your budget is tight, the home diffuser works wonderfully too. I'd also encourage you to sign up for Essential Rewards. You get to pick the oils that come to your door every single month. You switch them out; and you get paid 10% back for everything you order in reward points. That's 10% back on your laundry soap, dish soap, and Thieves cleaner (which is all I use to clean my house). It's one of the best choices I've ever made. If you'd like to add those to your order, I recommend the Thieves Essential Rewards kit, because in one swoop, it contains just about all you need to get rid of nearly every chemical cleaner in your home. It's simple and easy. If you're taking chemical-free living head on, it's the best place to start.

The final window asks for payment; and then you're off and running. We're honored to have you as a part of this team. Look for a welcome package in the mail! Connect with us online at Oil Ability with Sarah on Facebook. Find more resources at oilabilityteam. com. Welcome to our family!

This is something you NEED to take seriously. No one is watching your home but you. You are the gatekeeper. I'd be willing to bet my life that there are things in your home right now that you're exposed to every single day that could be killing you. The thing is, it's totally preventable.

What do you do until the box arrives?

Start small. Start slow. Start with what you're convicted on. Let me give you a simple tip. With your food, flip the bottles over and start reading the ingredients. If you can't pronounce it, don't eat it. It doesn't mean you can't have ice cream, just go for the ice cream with milk, sugar, eggs, and vanilla instead of an ingredients list of 35 items you don't recognize.

With your home, start with the biggest offenders first: laundry soap, dishwasher soap, cleaning supplies, candles, and plug-ins. Toss the candles and plug-ins. Swap them out with a diffuser and pure essential oil. Young Living has oil-infused Thieves cleaner, laundry soap, and dish soap that's affordable and simple to use. Add them to your Essential Rewards order once you have that Starter Kit.

This is about small, simple, baby steps. Take it one month at a time, as you swap things out in your home. Maybe the first month you focus solely on Thieves cleaner, and toss your cleaning supplies. You can start that today by grabbing a $22 bottle of Thieves cleaner. Go home and wipe your kitchen down and fall in love, knowing you just boosted your immune system instead of taxing your liver. Get a copy of the *Fearless* book when your kit arrives and start kicking chemicals to the curb one room at a time. It will take you through process step by step.

I started this journey myself with a Young Living starter kit and have never looked back. We use oils every single day in our home. Every oil you use is a chemical you're not using. It's not just an oils kit, it's a lifestyle.

You matter. Your family matters. Your friends matter. You can take control of your own health. Kick the chemicals out of your life and start living clean.

Get this as a textable class for free at:
oilabilityteam.com/share and "class."

7 Days of IPA's To Maintain Business Momentum: A Checklist

What's an IPA? It's an income-producing activity. It's an activity directly related to teaching classes, getting people on Essential Rewards, or training leaders. Do you need a quick checklist to make sure you're on track? Try this list. Frankly, I get overwhelmed with lists; and I get overwhelmed if I have too much to fill out. I prefer action over a lot of journaling. Promise me that you won't look at these as "must-do" items, but rather as a wish list; or a bucket list of business goals. If you cross one thing off in a day, you've done a great job. If you hit more, you're rock star status. The overall lesson is that you should not go a week without sharing oils. If you master that, toss these lists. Now, if you love lists and they keep you focused, when seven days are up, start with day one all over again.

Above all… never forget who you are! You are a ***#DIAMONDRISING!***

Day 1:

☐ Practice the 101 or 102 script in the mirror (with the bold close).

☐ Shoot a quick text to your five closest friends or family members asking to do a class; even if it's a one on one class. You want them as your level ones, even if they never build the business. You want to carry them with you as a financial blessing to their family. Ideally your level two's should be self-starters that carry the leg.

☐ Message one friend on social media and do not talk oils, just build relationships.

☐ Create an oils post on social media.

☐ Start making a list of your warm market, the people you know.

☐ Order starter kit fliers, 101 cd's, *Fearless* and the *Gameplan mini;* and prepare to assemble purple bags.

☐ Pray deliberately over your business.

Day 2:

☐ Give your first 101 class, even if it's with your mom or best friend only.

☐ Get dates on the calendar with the five friends you texted (see if you can get at least one class this week!)

☐ Plot out your personal monthly Essential Rewards order by thumbing through a reference guide and setting health goals.

☐ Message one friend on social media and do *not* talk oils, just build relationships.

☐ If it is the beginning of the month, announce the Young Living Essential Rewards promos.

☐ Add names to your warm market list.

☐ Write your personal story that you'll open all your classes with. Why do you oil? Share it.

☐ Pray deliberately over your business .

Day 3:

☐ Practice talking to your cold market. Strike up a conversation with a post office or gas station employee that is oils related. Start to develop a conscious eye of those around you in need.

☐ Add names to your warm market list.

☐ While you are waiting for your "first in-person class", teach an online class. Invite just a couple people to a Facebook Live in a private event. Keep it to 15-30 minutes and interact with them, reading the 101 or 102 script.

☐ Message one friend on social media and do *not* talk oils, just build relationships.

☐ Print off free materials at oilabilityteam.com to assemble purple bags.

☐ Pray deliberately over your business.

Day 4:

☐ Send a textable class (free at oilabilityteam.com) to five people on your warm market list that would be receptive to oils. After this, send texts to build the relationship first; then when the door opens, send the textable class. When they listen on their phones as a podcast, it's as if they sat in your living room and listened to you teach. A textable class is easy to send, just copy the link and paste in a text.

☐ Add names to your warm market list.

☐ Message one friend on social media and do *not* talk oils, just build relationships.

☐ Consider a volunteering opportunity through your church, your kid's school, or your community to network.

☐ Practice the art of follow up. Talk to the people who have responded online, attended a class, or were sent a textable class and ask this leading question: "what was your favorite part of the class?" "What would you love to learn more about?" "What is your greatest health struggle?" Use those leading questions to open the door to the premium starter kit.

☐ Pray deliberately over your business.

Day 5:

☐ Feeling discouraged? Go watch the free "Sarah's Why" video at oilabilityteam.com.

☐ Add names to your warm market list.

☐ Read *Fearless* and accept the *Fearless* challenges on the free 30-day printable calendar to learn more about oils. The more you expand your oils knowledge, the more you can share. Oil with purpose every day. If I'm having a rough day, I usually have forgotten to oil up. *Fearless* is a powerful training on how and why to oil. It's lifestyle training. Don't train the starter kit, train the lifestyle.

☐ Write down some stories you've experienced or heard of linked to the 12 oils in the starter kit. These will be stories you can share during your own 101. Facts tell... stories sell.

☐ Message one friend on social media and do *not* talk oils, just build relationships.

☐ Follow up and start an oils conversation with someone online that you've been building a relationship with.

☐ Pray deliberately over your business.

Day 6:

☐ Create an oils post on social media (to avoid scaring off your audience, four in every five posts should NOT be oils related).

☐ Assemble purple bags. 80-percent of your business is just being prepared for chance conversations and collecting the person's contact information. In my bags, I put a cover sheet (free at oilabilityteam.com), a photo of the kit on a flier, a 101 or *Toxin Free Life* (102) cd, *Fearless*, my business card, and instructions on how to join the team with my number as sponsor and enroller. I always keep five of these bags in my car, and give one to each person that attends a class.

☐ Add names to your warm market list and continue making contact with at least one person a day. Even if you never get past one a day, you'll be touching base with 30 new contacts a month. If you're building relationships, meeting needs, and listening; that's enough to build nearly to Silver in three months.

The average Silver has 100 members on their team. Stay focused, stay positive, and meet needs. If they are not ready for a 101, lead with Thieves and the 102 instead. Chemical free cleaning is almost always a common bond, especially when it's as affordable as Thieves.

☐ Follow up daily now. Continue conversations on social media instant messaging, via text, and by phone.

☐ Even if you spend 15 minutes a day touching base, it will lay a strong platform and foundation for your business. Following up is a critical skill that will save you as you start holding four to six classes a month; especially when they have their kit and you are lifestyle training to get them on Essential Rewards.

☐ Pray deliberately over your business.

Day 7:

☐ If you have not done one yet, teach an in-person class. At the 2019 Young Living International Grand Convention, one speaker said that 70-percent of all builders build their organization face to face. 30-percent use every other method out there: vendor events, textable classes, social media, etc.... No certain way is the wrong way to build. But try connecting with those around you, even if it's one person at a time, at least once a week. Two-thirds of my Silvers built to their rank in six months by holding four to six classes a month, consistently.

☐ Connect with one person today and either build a relationship or talk oils. (Need ideas? Print out your Facebook friend list, your Instagram, or Twitter list; and highlight all the names that are not on your team.)

☐ Follow up. Speak with a second person today where the foundation has been laid and talk oils. If they have come to a class, use my three leading questions above and ask about their interest in getting started with a starter kit. I like to use the sentence, "I believe this is the answer you've been looking for."

☐ Schedule classes for the rest of the month.

☐ Add names to your warm market list (I carry this list with me for 30 days constantly, then again once a week thereafter to keep adding names that I've forgotten).

☐ Pray deliberately over your business. Make three columns in a prayer journal: thanks, leaders, goals. Write down what's gone well this week. Write down the names of people who may be interested in joining you in the business. If there are no names, then pray for what you want in a leader and ask the Lord to bring them to your team. Write down your business goals and pray heartily over them.

WHAT ABOUT TRAINING LEADERS?

The IPA list will carry you far. It's got basic training on how to kick start the process of connecting with people (which will lead to teaching classes), as well as prompts for how to do follow up with confidence (get people on ER). The only missing piece is training leaders. For that, start with the Your *Gameplan: Build A Life Beyond Survival Mode.* I give the business opportunity in every class with this single sentence: "if you'd like to learn how to get your oils for free, read this mini, check that you're interested in the form I pass around on a clipboard, and I'll connect with you this week." That's it. (The form I just mentioned is a sheet of lined paper on a clipboard that asks them for their name and address, if they're interested in coming to another class, or if they want to learn how to get their oils for free.) The mini books I mentioned above go on every chair at every class I teach. They are quite different from this little *Ignite* book. They are for prospecting, and this book is for training. That book lights a fire. This book kindles it and gives you action steps to begin.

Once you connect and they have read the *Build A Life Beyond Survival Mode* mini, the next step is this *Ignite* mini. You can have them trained, off the ground, and duplicating in a single afternoon. Once they are actively building, if they want deeper training, the *Gameplan* book, *Gameplan workbook,* and full 12-day free bootcamp are online. I personally run *Gameplan* bootcamps twice a year with my team in January and July, and they always lead to OGV growth.

Got all that?

- **Step 1:** *Your Gameplan: Build A Life Beyond Survival Mode* **(prospecting)**

- **Step 2:** *Ignite* mini **(training)**

- **Step 3:** *Gameplan book and workbook + bootcamp* **(ready for more)**

Discount
Get the *Ignite* Mini

You will be able to train your leaders for $5 each!

This is a powerful gift
for new builders and rank up recognition!

KEEP YOUR LEADERS LASER FOCUSED ON:

- ♟ Teaching classes
- ♟ Training the lifestyle through ER
- ♟ Launching their own leaders with "Ignite"

SNAG BOOKS ON THE OILABILITYTEAM.COM WEBSITE.

Made in the USA
Middletown, DE
05 July 2019